Instructor's Manual and Test Bank

to accompany

Reconstructing Gender
A Multicultural Anthology

Third Edition

Estelle Disch
University of Massachusetts, Boston

Prepared by
Estelle Disch
University of Massachusetts, Boston

Kristine M. De Welde
University of Colorado at Boulder

Boston   Burr Ridge, IL   Dubuque, IA   Madison, WI   New York   San Francisco   St. Louis
Bangkok   Bogotá   Caracas   Kuala Lumpur   Lisbon   London   Madrid   Mexico City
Milan   Montreal   New Delhi   Santiago   Seoul   Singapore   Sydney   Taipei   Toronto

Instructor's Manual and Test Bank to accompany
RECONSTRUCTING GENDER
Estelle Disch

Published by McGraw-Hill, an imprint of The McGraw-Hill Companies, Inc., 1221 Avenue of the Americas,
New York, NY 10020. Copyright © 2003 (2000) by The McGraw-Hill Companies, Inc.

2 3 4 5 6 7 8 9 0 QSR/QSR 0 9 8 7 6 5 4

ISBN 0-7674-2773-4

www.mhhe.com

CONTENTS

PART IX: VIOLENCE   68

Questions on the Introduction to Part IX   68

PART X: HEALTH AND ILLNESS   76

Questions on the Introduction to Part X   76

PART XI: A WORLD THAT IS TRULY HUMAN   85

Questions on the Introduction to Part XI   85

SECTION II: QUESTIONS FOR CLASSROOM DISCUSSIONS, READING JOURNALS, OR TAKE-HOME ESSAY EXAMS   95

GENERAL INTRODUCTION   95

PART I: SOCIAL CONTEXTS OF GENDER   96

PART X: HEALTH AND ILLNESS   119

PART XI: A WORLD THAT IS TRULY HUMAN   121

SECTION I: MULTIPLE CHOICE, TRUE/FALSE, AND SHORT ANSWER QUESTIONS

GENERAL INTRODUCTION

Multiple Choice

1. Which of the following intellectual perspectives does NOT form a basis for this book?
   a. The sociological imagination
   b. The commitment to understand the experiences of people who are frequently excluded from academic discourse
   *c. The central importance of canonical literature
   d. The reconstruction of knowledge

Pages 1–10[1]

2. According to Disch, C. Wright Mills argued that
   a. people need to understand themselves in historical context in order to make sense of their lives.
   b. people need to distinguish between personal troubles and public issues in order to understand the sources of their problems.
   *c. a and b.
   d. Neither a nor b.

Page 2

3. "The personal is political" is a slogan adopted by
   *a. the second wave of the feminist movement.
   b. C. Wright Mills.
   c. Robert K. Merton.
   d. All of the above.

Page 2

4. The sociological imagination helps us to do all of the following EXCEPT:
   *a. understand the psychopathology of events like September 11th.
   b. understand how the complex realms of international trade influence events.
   c. understand the historical context of a particular event.
   d. understand how issues of foreign policy impact individual lives.

Page 3

5. The phrase "intersecting identities" refers to
   a. the melting pot of diverse ethnicities in the United States.
   *b. the presence in individuals of multiple traits that contribute to their complex identities.
   c. the complex needs of constituents that must be addressed by people running for public office.
   d. the importance in men's studies of studying men as men.

---

[1]Page numbers are provided except in cases where the question addresses most or all of a particular reading.

Pages 9-10

6. According to the author of the text, work in men's studies does NOT typically include
    a. dissatisfaction with men's roles.
    b. attention to the experiences of a wide range of men.
    *c. a commitment to establishing new roles for men in which they would be more appropriately attentive to women's traditional needs.
    d. awareness of men's power over other men.

Pages 8-9

7. Which of the following is NOT a basic error in knowledge, according to Elizabeth Minnich?
    a. Overgeneralization
    b. Attachment to mystified concepts
    c. Circular reasoning
    *d. Systematic attention to inclusivity

Pages 12-13

8. Which of the following is NOT an example of a participant in the Trans liberation movement, according to Leslie Feinberg?
    *a. Hypermasculine men
    b. Cross-dressers
    c. Intersexuals
    d. Transsexuals

Page 6

True/False

9. Disch suggests that expected standards of masculinity might attempt to impose on males expressions of feelings, open communication, and "good behavior." (True, page 4)

10. According to Disch, public homophobia seems to be softening a bit here in the U.S. as well as abroad. (True, page 5)

11. The gender system affects both men and women in equivalent ways. (False, page 8)

12. The tendency of men to challenge the "be tough, take-charge, don't feel" way of being men is usually referred to as hegemonic masculinity. (False, page 8)

13. According to Elizabeth Janeway, "disbelief" includes the refusal to accept the definition of oneself put forth by those with more power. (True, page 17)

14. Marilyn Frye, using the metaphor of a bird cage to characterize oppression, argues that careful and close examination of any bar of the cage can provide an effective handle for understanding the full picture of oppression. (False, pages 14-15)

15. Trans liberation includes such people as feminine women, masculine men, cross-dressers, and intersexuals. (False, page 6)

PART I: SOCIAL CONTEXTS OF GENDER

QUESTIONS ON THE INTRODUCTION TO PART I

Multiple Choice

1. Whereas our biological makeup is usually referred to as _____, the social expectations for male and female behavior are usually referred to as _____.
    a. hormonally based; butch-femme
    *b. sex; gender
    c. instinctual; inherited
    d. immutable; unchangeable

Page 28

True/False

2. In every known society, social institutions shape the expectations of how women and men should behave. (True, page 27)

3. Individuals who are fully committed to changing gender expectations have relative freedom to do so in the United States. (False, page 27)

4. As individuals, we have the power to change social structures by stretching the rules of conformity. (False, page 27)

Reading 1
TOWARD BLACK AMERICAN EMPOWERMENT
Manning Marable

Multiple Choice

1. According to Marable, in spite of the end of Jim Crow legislation, members of the Black middle class were NOT able to
    a. integrate many professions.
    b. escape the confines of the ghetto.
    *c. support the upward mobility of blue collar Blacks.
    d. integrate white suburbs.

Page 31

2. According to Marable, the "epidemic" of violence in the Black community is caused by
    a. unemployment.
    b. poor health care.
    c. inadequate housing.
    *d. All of the above.

Pages 30-31

3. The most frequent victims of rape are

3

a. white women.
*b. Black women.
c. Black children.
d. white children.

Page 32

4. The most frequent kind of homicide is
   *a. a Black man killing a Black man.
   b. a white man killing a Black man.
   c. a Black man killing a white man.
   d. a white man killing a white woman.

Page 33

5. Which of the following is the major cause of the crisis in the Black community, according to Marable?
   a. An educational system that ignores the accomplishments of African Americans
   b. Internal violence in the Black community
   c. Negative labeling of Black children
   *d. The wider capitalist political economy characterized by institutional racism and class exploitation

Page 36

6. Marable suggests _____ as a strategy for mobilization.
   a. having more Black politicians
   *b. accountability measures for current politicians
   c. boycotts
   d. increased segregation of Black communities

Pages 38-39

True/False

7. According to Marable, the activism characteristic of the 1950s and 1960s is no longer necessary for the achievement of African American equality. (False, pages 30-31)

8. According to Marable, most middle-class Blacks have, in the interest of Black unity and civil rights, remained connected to poorer Black communities. (False, page 31)

9. According to Marable, the real unemployment rate for young Black men in cities is at least 50%. (True, page 34)

10. Although poor white women are much more likely to be raped than those with higher income, a similar class difference does not apply to Black women who are equally likely to be raped no matter what their income. (False, page 33)

11. Given that over 6,000 African Americans hold public office, Marable sees electoral politics as an effective means of bringing empowerment to the African American community. (False, pages 30, 39)

12. Marable calls for a collective commitment from all African Americans, regardless of class, to bring an end to the crisis in the Black community. (True, page 39)

4

Short Answer/Essay

13. How does Marable make sense of the rhetoric of equality in the face of persistent racism?

14. Discuss the connections between identity and violence as Marable presents them.

Reading 2
FROM NOTHING A CONSCIOUSNESS
Helen Zia

Multiple Choice

1. In order to start a dialogue about women in the Vietnam war, Zia used which of these experiences to talk about women and war?
    a. Her own experiences as a Vietnamese woman
    *b. Her mother's experiences in China
    c. Her family's experiences fleeing Japan
    d. None of the above.

Page 44

2. Zia did NOT find support in:
    a. other Asian women.
    b. White women.
    c. Asian men.
    *d. b and c.
    e. All of the above.

Page 45

True/False

3. Most of the Asian-Americans activists whom Zia worked with limited their scope to Asian-American issues of civil liberties. (False, page 43)

4. Zia found it difficult to confront sexist Asian professors because of their shared ethnicity. (True, page 45)

Short Answer/Essay

5. What were some of Zia's college experiences that led to her activism?

6. Compare your own college activist activities to Zia's. What similar (or different) obstacles have you faced?

Reading 3
THE PUERTO RICAN DUMMY AND THE MERCIFUL SON
Martín Espada

1. Espada contains his anger by
   *a. writing.
   b. punching lamps.
   c. street fighting.
   d. All of the above.

Page 49

2. A way that Espada expects to help his son not be violent is
   a. urging his son to be a pacifist.
   *b. modeling respectful treatment of his wife.
   c. teaching his son about honor.
   d. All of the above.

Page 50

3. Which is NOT a characteristic of the contemporary men's movement, according to Espada?
   *a. Thoughtful self-criticism
   b. Racism
   c. Use of Native American symbols
   d. A self-congratulatory tone

Page 54

True/False

4. Espada hopes to bring his son into the men's movement that he identifies with. (False, page 54)

5. Espada argues that although sexist and violent behavior characterizes Anglo as well as Latino men, the presence of machismo in Latino culture emphasizes these traits and raises sexism and violence to a more intense level. (False, page 55)

6. Espada expresses his personhood by refusing to live out the stereotypical behavior expected of Puerto Rican men. (True, whole essay)

7. Espada acknowledges that Latino male behavior is often more sexist and violent than Anglo men's behavior. (False, page 55)

Short Answer/Essay

8. What has happened to Espada and what has he done to lead him to say the following? "My evolving manhood was defined by how well I could take punishment, and paradoxically I punished myself for not being man enough to end my own humiliation." (page 48)

6

Reading 4
ANGRY WOMEN ARE BUILDING
Issues and Struggles Facing American Indian Women Today

Paula Gunn Allen

Multiple Choice

1. According to Paula Gunn Allen, the major issue for American Indian women today is
    *a. survival of American Indian people.
    b. dealing with rape.
    c. the decline in the status of women within American Indian tribes.
    d. high rates of alcoholism.

Page 57

2. Unemployment among American Indians is approximately _____.
    a. 20 %
    b. 35 %
    c. 50 %
    *d. 60 % or higher

Page 57

3. Allen argues that a major cause of violence against American Indian women by American Indian men is
    *a. depictions of American Indian men in the media.
    b. urbanization.
    c. industrialization.
    d. men's use of alcohol.

Page 59

True/False

4. Allen suggests that around 25% of Indian women have been sterilized without their consent. (True, page 57)

5. Allen suggests that a solution to many of the problems of American Indians might be to better assimilate into Anglo culture. (False, page 60)

Short Answer/ Essay

6. Discuss some of the survival issues mentioned by Allen in her discussion of the lives of American Indian women.

Reading 5
"J.A.P."-SLAPPING
The Politics of Scapegoating
Ruth Atkin and Adrienne Rich

Multiple Choice

1. Atkin and Rich argue that the stereotype of the "Jewish-American Princess" is based on
   a. anti-Semitic attitudes.
   b. sexism both within and outside the Jewish community.
   c. racist attitudes toward people of Japanese descent.
   *d. All of the above.

Pages 61-64

2. Atkin and Rich argue that "J.A.P." stereotypes are linked to an economy in which the gap between rich and poor
   *a. is widening.
   b. is shrinking.
   c. is holding steady.
   d. is almost nonexistent.

Page 63

3. The "J.A.P." label is often applied to:
   a. Jewish women only.
   b. Asian women only.
   c. Jewish and Asian women.
   d. spoiled, self-indulgent women.
   *e. All of the above.

Pages 63-64

True/False

4. Atkin and Rich argue that a possible explanation for the scapegoating of women in a historically scapegoated group is tension over gender roles in the group. (True, page 62)

Reading 6
TO BE POOR AND TRANSGENDER
Kai Wright

Multiple Choice

1. One of the Primary needs for transgender/transitioning individuals, according to Kai is:
   a. support groups.
   b. medications.
   *c. counseling.
   d. housing.

2. The clinical term for transgender is:
    *a.   gender identity disorder.
    b.   gender malady complex.
    c.   borderline gender disorder.
    d.   gender polarity complex.

Page 66

True/False

3. Many transgender professionals feel that having a medical diagnosis for their gender dysphoria is helpful. (False, page 66)

4. Most transgender people who have "passing privilege" seek out being an activist or role model. (False, page 69)

Short Answer/ Essay

5. Describe some of the issues that the transgender community faces.

Reading 7
WHITE PRIVILEGE AND MALE PRIVILEGE
A Personal Account of Coming to See Correspondence through Work in Women's Studies

Peggy McIntosh

Multiple Choice

1. Peggy McIntosh, in "White Privilege: Unpacking the Invisible Knapsack" states that it is difficult to see white privilege because:
    a.   it is often embedded in invisible systems of domination.
    b.   Americans are taught to define racism as overt acts of meanness.
    c.   Americans are taught that they earn their place in society based on their individual merit and moral will.
    *d.   All of the above.

Pages 72, 79

2. According to Peggy McIntosh, in "White Privilege: Unpacking the Invisible Knapsack" which of the following is TRUE?
    *a.   Interlocking oppressions take both active and embedded forms.
    b.   The list of conditions are things that Black people can count on in our society.
    c.   Most white people perceive white as a racial identity.
    d.   People earn their place in society based on their individual ability and will.
    e.   The invisible knapsack is useful for spies who want to backpack incognito.

Page 79

3. Whiteness is:
    a. assimilation into White culture.
    *b. a racial identity.
    c. the privilege given to Blacks who are light-skinned.
    d. the oppression of Whites.

Page 78

4. The myth of meritocracy is the myth that:
    a. if you get good grades you will get a job.
    b. the social merits of being white outweigh the negative aspects.
    *c. democratic choice is equally available to all.
    d. people of color work hardest to succeed.

Pages 79-80

True/False

5. Earned strength and unearned power are essentially very similar, according to McIntosh. (False, page 77)

6. McIntosh argues that different oppressions have similar advantages associated with them. (False, page 79)

Short Answer/Essay

7. Choose five of McIntosh's privilege conditions that you identify with and discuss why.

8. What are some things that have contributed to your own positive life experiences that you did not earn?

9. McIntosh discusses white and heterosexual privilege (as well as male privilege). Using a similar argument, discuss class privilege.

Reading 8
THEORIZING DIFFERENCE FROM MULTIRACIAL FEMINISM
Maxine Baca Zinn and Bonnie Thornton Dill

Multiple Choice

1. The most central issue in the thinking of Zinn and Dill is
    a. acknowledging the wide range of differences among women.
    b. finding common ground among women of all groups.
    *c. examining the role of race in women's lives.
    d. All of the above.

Pages 83-84, plus whole article

2. According to Zinn and Dill, race and class are especially crucial areas of analysis because
    a. they are differences that are often ignored.

b. they make clear how intersections between differences can occur.

c. they help to universalize women.

*d. they are primary organizing principles of U.S society and determine both individuals' and groups' opportunities.

Page 82

3. According to Zinn and Dill, which of the following is NOT a characteristic of multiracial feminism?

a. It examines how multiple aspects of the social order simultaneously affect people's experiences.

b. It highlights the relationship between women with power and those without power (e.g., white women and women of color).

c. It explores how women have empowered themselves in the face of race, class, and gender oppression.

*d. It addresses the particular needs of men and women of color so that their lives can be examined in careful detail without reference to other groups.

Pages 86-87

4. A limitation of socialist feminist thinking, according to Zinn and Dill, is its failure to adequately address

*a. race.

b. class.

c. homophobia.

d. ableism.

Page 85

5. Multiracial feminism builds upon, yet is distinct from:

a. women's studies and race and ethnic studies.

*b. socialist feminism and race and ethnic studies.

c. socialist feminism and women's studies.

d. race and ethnic studies and lesbian/bisexual/gay studies.

Pages 84-85

True/False

6. Zinn and Dill argue that differences among women are overemphasized and that acknowledging the level of commonality among women is necessary in order to organize for women's rights. (False, page 87)

7. According to Zinn and Dill, a major tension in contemporary feminism is the conflict between those who search for universal aspects that characterize women and those who acknowledge that universal aspects might not exist. (True, pages 82-83)

Short Answer/Essay

8. Discuss several ways multiracial feminism is different from and similar to contemporary feminism.

Part II: GENDER SOCIALIZATION
QUESTIONS ON THE INTRODUCTION TO PART II

Multiple Choice

1. An example of how gender behavior changes in different situations is illustrated by
   a. children in the Dominican Republic whose genitalia change at adolescence.
   b. middle-class women who worked in factories during World War II and then returned home to work as housewives and mothers after the war.
   c. the case of a castrated male infant who was raised as a girl and later became male.
   *d. All of the above.

Pages 92-93

2. The case of "John" and "Joan" suggests that
   a. efforts to reassign the sex of a child who is genetically and hormonally normal are likely to be unsuccessful.
   b. people can change their gender if they feel compelled to do so.
   c. a man can live a satisfactory life without a normal penis.
   *d. All of the above.

Pages 92-93

3. Increased gender equality has led to the following EXCEPT:
   a. higher math and science scores for girls.
   b. higher rates of smoking for girls.
   c. higher rates of drinking and drugs for girls.
   *d. higher rates of suicide for boys.

Page 92

True/False

4. The genes that determine sex come in exactly two combinations. (False, page 91)

5. The hormonal makeup and physical characteristics of humans fall along a continuum defined as masculine at one end and feminine on the other. (True, page 91)

6. Men and women typically grow more similar in midlife. (True, page 93)

Reading 9
THE SOCIAL CONSTRUCTION OF GENDER
Judith Lorber

Multiple Choice

1. A sex category becomes a gender status through
   a. naming.
   b. dress.
   c. different treatment of boys and girls.

*d.   All of the above.

Page 97

2.   According to Lorber, as part of _____, gender ranks men above women of the same race and class.
    a.   an educational system
    b.   a socialization system
    c.   a normative system
    *d.   a stratification system

Page 98

3.   According to Lorber, a factor that contributes to men's control over better-paid jobs is
    *a.   the active gendering of jobs and people, such that the better-paid jobs get defined as men's jobs.
    b.   men's physical strength.
    c.   women's lack of desire for such jobs.
    d.   All of the above.

Pages 99-100

4.   Lorber concludes that the continuing purpose of gender as a modern social institution is
    a.   to organize the labor force in ways that allow for child rearing from generation to generation.
    *b.   to construct women as a group to be the subordinates of men as a group.
    c.   to reinforce homophobia and heterosexism.
    d.   All of the above.

Page 101

5.   According to Lorber, gender inequality is produced by
    a.   sex and anatomy.
    b.   procreation and hormones.
    c.   genetic predispositions across various cultures.
    *d.   None of the above.

True/False

6.   Lorber provides a number of examples of gender bending in order to illustrate how gender is disappearing. (False, pages 96-97)

7.   Lorber points out that gender norms are maintained only by informal sanctions, not by formal sanctions. (False, page 98)

Short Answer/Essay

8.   What does Lorber mean by "Resistance and rebellion have altered gender norms, but so far they have rarely eroded the statuses"? (page 98)

9.   What does Lorber mean when she quotes Judith Butler as saying that "not biology, but culture, becomes destiny"? (page 101)

10. What does Lorber mean when she argues that gender is socially constructed?

11. What does Lorber mean by gender as a process AND a structure? (pages 98-101)

MASCULINITY AS HOMOPHOBIA

Michael S. Kimmel

Multiple Choice

1. According to Kimmel, the vast majority of men in the United States are disempowered by one or more of the following EXCEPT
   a.   ethnic and racial prejudice.
   b.   poverty.
   c.   homophobia.
   *d.   reverse racism.

Page 108

2. According to Kimmel, "_____ is the fear that other men will unmask us, emasculate us, reveal to us and the world that we do not measure up, that we are not real men."
   a.   Insecurity
   *b.   Homophobia
   c.   Locker room harassment
   d.   Competition

Page 104

3. According to Kimmel, men's feelings of powerlessness emerge from the discontinuity between _____ and _____.
   *a.   the social; the psychological
   b.   their hormones; social expectations
   c.   their impulses toward violence; their inability to control their impulses
   d.   their need for other men; their fear of loving men

Pages 106-107

4. According to Kimmel, _____ is a central organizing principle of the U.S. definition of manhood.
   a.   testosterone
   b.   violence
   *c.   homophobia
   d.   All of the above.

Page 103

5. In a survey cited by Kimmel, men reported being most afraid of
   *a.   being laughed at.
   b.   reverse discrimination.
   c.   being physically overpowered by other men.
   d.   being called a sissy.

Page 106

True/False

6. According to Kimmel, middle-class straight white men maintain a sense of superiority by excluding gay men, men of color, women, and men born outside the United States. (True, pages 108)

7. Kimmel thinks that many men in the United States are frustrated and angry because they were raised to believe themselves entitled to power but do not, in reality, feel powerful. (True, page 107)

8. According to Kimmel, men are most threatened by the negative judgments of women. (False, page 103)

Short Answer/Essay

9. According to Kimmel, how is it that men can be both powerful and powerless?

Reading 11
BOYHOOD, ORGANIZED SPORTS, AND THE CONSTRUCTION OF MASCULINITIES

Michael A. Messner

Multiple Choice

1. Which of the following best describes the focus of Messner's research?
    *a. A study of former athletes' lives
    b. A study of men's relationships with their fathers
    c. A study of men's difficulties with intimacy
    d. A study of the impact of competition on men's development

Page 111

2. Messner argues that gender identity
    a. is an aspect of personality established in childhood that remains more or less constant throughout life.
    *b. is a process that develops and changes throughout life.
    c. is closely tied to instincts and physiology.
    d. None of the above.

Page 110

3. The _____ of the men Messner interviewed seemed to affect how important sports were in their overall identities.
    a. family structure
    b. age
    *c. social status
    d. All of the above.

Pages 120-124

True/False

4. The men interviewed by Messner described loneliness, insecurity and a need to connect with other people as reasons why men played sports in childhood. (True, page 117)

5. Older brothers were typically in the role of exposing the men interviewed to sports or pushing them into sports. (False, page 115)

6. Messner concludes that the combination of intimacy and distance that accompanies organized sports fits the needs of many men. (True, pages 188-119)

7. The social order so carefully dictates gender that there is little room for personal creativity or individual input into the process. (False, pages 110-111)

Short Answer/Essay

8. Compare and contrast a male athlete you know with the men interviewed by Messner on the issues of his relationship with his father, his identity as a man, and his career aspirations.

10. What does Messner mean when he argues that gender identity is socially constructed?

11. What is the role of fathers in boys' involvement with sports?

12. Discuss Messner's connections between class and sports achievement in relation to masculine identity.

Reading 12
COLOR, HAIR TEXTURE AND STANDARDS OF BEAUTY
Patricia Hill Collins

True/False

1. Collins suggests that judging white women by their looks objectifies AND privileges them. (True, page 128)

2. Dividing African-Americans into two categories according to their skin's lightness/darkness affects dark-skinned and light-skinned women very similarly. (False, pages 129-130)

Short Answer/Essay

3. Collins argues that within the binary thinking that supports oppressions, the dominant could not exist without the other. Discuss what you think she means.

4. What does Collins mean by "colorism?" (page 128)

Reading 13
THE MYTH OF THE LATIN WOMAN
I Just Met a Girl Named Maria
Judith Ortiz Cofer

Multiple Choice

1. Cofer's essay is primarily about
   *a. stereotypes of Latina women.
   b. "cute" behavior by Anglo men toward Latina women.
   c. dress customs of Latino women and men.
   d. street poems (*piropos*) composed by Latino men.

True/False

2. Stereotypes of Latina women contribute to keeping many of them in low-status jobs such as domestic workers. (True, page 135)

3. Cofer says she has been spared many hardships related to stereotypes of Latina women because of her education. (True, page 136)

Short Answer/Essay

4. Name some of the areas of miscommunication between Latina women and people in mainstream U.S. culture, as described by Cofer.

Reading 14
HE DEFIES YOU STILL
The Memoirs of a Sissy
Tommi Avicolli

Multiple Choice

1. Which of the following changes does Avicolli NOT identify as a strategy to make schools more welcoming to boys labeled "sissies"?
   a. Teachers who intervene to stop harassment
   b. Teaching about the contributions of gay people to society
   c. Teaching that homosexuals are not pathetic and sick
   *d. Gay-straight alliances in schools

2. Avicolli talks about coping with his sense of powerlessness by doing all of the following EXCEPT
   a. writing.
   *b. doing well in school.
   c. attending a gay pride march.
   d. hiding from bullies.

Page 138

17

True/False

3. Avicolli found empowerment by rebelling in high school and confronting the priest who pressed upon him the importance of relating to girls. (False, page 125)

4. Luckily, Avicolli's parents were accepting of his "difference" from other boys. (False, page 140)

Short Answer/Essay

5. In what ways is Avicolli's experience familiar to you and in what ways is it unfamiliar? Use examples of rejection incidents that happened either to you or to people around you during your years in school. To what extent did you participate in teasing others?

Reading 15
GROWING UP HIDDEN
Linnea Due

Multiple Choice

1. Due likens pretending to be heterosexual to:
    a. putting on a Halloween costume.
    b. cross-dressing.
    *c. learning a foreign language.
    d. being a ghost.

Page 143

2. Due coped with her hidden self by:
    a. running away from home.
    b. sleeping around.
    *c. drinking heavily.
    d. dropping out of school.

Pages 143

True/False

3. Due was open about her sexuality only with her closest friends. (False, pages 143-144)

Reading 16
THE MILITARY AS A SECOND BAR MITZVAH
Combat Service As Initiation to Zionist Masculinity

Danny Kaplan

Multiple Choice

1. Nir, the man Kaplan focuses his article on:
    a. considers combat an experience of ecstasy.
    b. questions the very notion of combat.
    c. dehumanizes those he shoots.
    *d. all of the above.

Pages 149-150

True/False

2. In order to maintain solidarity, the IDF recruits only from very specific sectors of society. (False, page 145)

3. According to Kaplan, the IDF is the dominant socializing agent in Isreal. (True, page 145)

4. Serving in the IDF is mandatory for both men and women. (True, page 145)

5. Nir is fully indoctrinated into the military ideology. (False, page 148)

Short Answer/Essay

6. What is the relationship between culture/nationalism, masculinity and sexual orientation according to Kaplan's research?

Reading 17
MALE GENDER AND RITUALS OF RESISTANCE IN THE PALESTINIAN INTIFADA
A Cultural Politics of Violence

Julie Peteet

Multiple Choice

1. According to Peteet, beatings suffered by young men:
    *a. empower the individual.
    b. break the individual down.
    c. create solidarity among soldiers.
    d. are effective ways of converting soldiers to the "other" side.

Page 157

True/False

2. According to Peteet, men who suffer beatings when detained have status in their communities when they are released. (True, page 156)

3. Respect is shown to a beaten youth in Palestinian society. (True, page 157)

Short Answer/Essay

4. Why is Palestinian prison considered a "school" or "university?"

5. What are some ways which a previously imprisoned youth is shown respect?

6. Why is enduring physical violence honored by Palestinian communities?

Part III: EMBODIMENT

QUESTIONS ON THE INTRODUCTION TO PART III

Multiple Choice

1. Female athletes are much more easily accepted if they
   - a. are slim and muscular.
   - *b. appear to be feminine.
   - c. deny their eating disorders.
   - d. All of the above.

   Page 162

2. Women who look too athletic are threatening because they
   - *a. challenge the division of the world into male and female.
   - b. provoke jealousy in other women.
   - c. don't look like acceptable mother figures.
   - d. All of the above.

   Page 162

3. According to a recent TV documentary, of 40,000 women who applied to a modeling agency, only ___ were found to be acceptable.
   - *a. four
   - b. twenty
   - c. one hundred
   - d. one hundred and fifty

   Page 163

4. An example of racially specific plastic surgery cited in the text is
   - a. white men getting "male enhancement" surgery to enlarge their penises.
   - b. liposuction among white women.
   - *c. nasal surgery among Asian women.
   - d. All of the above.

   Page 160

5. Approximately how often is a baby born whose sex is not obvious by looking at its genitals?
   - a. 1 in 500 births
   - *b. 1 in 1,500 births
   - c. 1 in 2,500 births
   - d. 1 in 3,500 births

   Page 162

6. The demand for plastic surgery has led to:
   - *a. underground beauty treatments performed by unlicensed practitioners.
   - b. a booming economy as a result of all the unnecessary surgeries.
   - c. millions of deaths as a result of liposuction complications.
   - d. all of the above.

   Page 161

7. The vast majority of people will look unacceptable by dominant societal standards because of growing old. (True, page 161)

8. Hymen reconstruction surgery has become more popular as the pressure to maintain virginity until marriage has increased. (True, page 161)

8. It is possible for a woman with a Y (male) chromosome to give birth. (True, pages 162-163)

10. Disch argues that it is a positive thing that the National Institutes of Health has lowered the point at which a person is defined as overweight since this will lead to healthier lifestyles. (False, page 163)

Reading 18
BEAUTY IS THE BEAST
Psychological Effects of the Pursuit of the Perfect Female Body

Elayne A. Saltzberg and Joan C. Chrisler

Multiple Choice

1. A group in which the rate of smoking is increasing is
   a. young men.
   *b. young women.
   c. women during menopause (to curb appetite).
   d. All of the above.

Page 170

2. Approximately what percentage of people in the United States with anorexia nervosa are women?
   a. 35%
   b. 55%
   c. 75%
   *d. 95%

Page 172

3. Approximately what percentage of diets fails?
   a. 35%
   b. 55%
   c. 75%
   *d. 95%

Page 171

4. Approximately what percentage of college-age women uses vomiting as a means of weight control?
   a. 10%
   b. 20%
   *c. 30%
   d. 40%

5. Which is NOT a result of striving to achieve the beauty ideal?
   a.   stress
   b.   anxiety
   *c.   higher self-esteem
   d.   weakened sense of self

True/False

6. According to the authors, attractiveness is a prerequisite for femininity, but not for masculinity. (True, page 167)

7. In spite of the pressure on women to conform to beauty ideals, the rate of plastic surgery is higher for men due to their higher rates of athletic injuries and accidents. (False, page 170)

8. Although anorexia nervosa is a serious condition, deaths from it are rare. (False, page 172)

9. While men typically engage in exercise to increase cardiovascular fitness, women do so to build body mass. (False, page 172)

10. Women defined as beautiful by society are less likely to feel unhappy about their looks than are less-attractive women. (False, page 173)

11. Landlords are less likely to rent to obese people. (True, page 174)

12. Saltzberg and Chrisler would appreciate a world in which women did not spend immense amounts of money and emotional energy on adapting to public ideals of beauty. (True, page 174)

Short Answer/Essay

13. Choose an example of obsession with beauty described by Saltzberg and Chrisler and compare/contrast it to the life of someone you know well.

14. If you know a woman who seems free of the beauty obsession, what do you think explains her freedom?

Reading 19

"A WAY OUTA NO WAY"

Eating Problems among African American, Latina, and White Women

Becky W. Thompson

Multiple Choice

1. Thompson reevaluates the interpretation of eating troubles as _____ based in
   _____.

   a.   psychological symptoms; early emotional conflict

    *b.   issues of appearance; the culture of thinness
     c.   transitory; normal life crises
     d.   All of the above.

Page 178

2. Diagnosis of eating problems is often delayed among women of color because
     a.   women of color have less access to medical care.
     b.   women of color have different eating patterns than do white women.
    *c.   professionals don't expect women of color to have eating troubles.
     d.   All of the above.

Page 179

3. Thompson's research is innovative in that it
    *a.   looks at the impact of intersecting oppressions on eating problems.
     b.   pays attention primarily to compulsive eating rather than to anorexia.
     c.   is restricted to women of color.
     d.   All of the above.

Page 180

4. The women Thompson interviewed related which of the following traumas most frequently to their eating difficulties?
     a.   Heterosexism
     b.   Poverty
     c.   Racism and/or classism
    *d.   Sexual abuse

Page 182

True/False

5. Although the women Thompson interviewed were affected to some extent by the pressures to be thin, they were more likely to have been affected by other factors. (True, page 189)

6. Thompson argues that although many issues affect women's eating problems, the pressures to be thin in U.S. culture dominate over other pressures and stresses. (False, pages 189)

Short Answer/Essay

7. What is Thompson's main contribution to explaining the eating troubles of women of color and white lesbians?

8. Discuss the connections between eating disorders and sexual abuse, as presented by Thompson.

Reading 20
JUST WALK ON BY
A Black Man Ponders His Power to Alter Public Space

Brent Staples

Multiple Choice

1. Which of the following is NOT used by Staples in his efforts to diffuse fear of him as a tall Black man?
   a. Whistling Vivaldi
   *b. Using verbal confrontations only with the police
   c. Leaving a wide berth around people on subway platforms
   d. Choosing not to follow people into buildings

Pages 195-196

True/False

2. Staples agrees that the threat he poses to pedestrians results from the reality of many Black men as criminals. (True, 194)

Reading 21
TAKING IT

Leonard Kriegel

Multiple Choice

1. Which of the following was not named by Kriegel as helping him fight his war with polio?
   a. Toughness
   b. Resilience
   c. Independence
   *d. Surrendering

True/False

2. Kriegel argues that polio is a gendered disease, to be fought by acting like a "man." (True, pages 196-197)

Short Answer/Essay

3. What are the connections Kriegel makes between his coping with polio and masculinity?

Reading 22
DO YOU REMEMBER ME?
Barbara Macdonald

Multiple Choice

1. Which of the following does NOT characterize Macdonald's experience of growing old?
    *a. Ambivalence about her "dumpy" body
    b. Accepting death
    c. Commitment to her partner
    d. All of the above.

Page 201

True/False

2. MacDonald writes about her struggle with growing old and how she is trapped by the beauty ideal in an older woman's body. (False, whole article)

Reading 23
I'M NOT FAT, I'M LATINA
Christy Haubegger

Multiple Choice

1. Haubegger's piece primarily addresses
    *a. the importance of cultural context in definitions of health and beauty.
    b. the medical establishment's campaign against women who are overweight.
    c. racism in the medical professions.
    d. All of the above.

True/False

2. Haubegger describes the pathological relationship Latino/a culture has with food. (False, page 203)

Short Answer/Essay

3. Discuss some of the experiences that have led Christy Haubegger to embrace her round body.

Reading 24
THE TYRANNY OF THE ESTHETIC:
Surgery's Most Intimate Violation

Martha Coventry

Multiple Choice

1. According to Martha Coventry, the main cause of suicidal feelings among people who have had genital surgery is
   a. the sense of difference from other children.
   b. physical pain following surgery.
   *c. loneliness.
   d. All of the above.

Page 207

2. In Coventry's opinion, sex reassignment surgery is typically performed
   a. for the physical health of the child.
   b. for the emotional health of the child.
   *c. because U.S. culture is not able to deal with people whose bodies are not obviously male or female.
   d. All of the above.

Page 210

3. Coventry compares sex reassignment surgery to
   *a. female genital mutilation in Africa.
   b. elective surgery by transsexuals.
   c. the transgender movement's quest for freedom of gender expression.
   d. All of the above.

Pages 209-210

True/False

4. A boy with a penis defined as "too small" by physicians is likely to have his penis converted to a clitoris and be reassigned female by physicians. (True, pages 210-211)

5. Female genital mutilation is different from sex reassignment surgery, according to Coventry, because the latter is done for humanitarian reasons whereas the former is not. (False, pages 209-210)

Short Answer/Essay

6. What does Coventry suggest as solutions to unnecessary genital surgery?

Reading 25
THE BURKA AND THE BIKINI
Joan Jacobs Brumberg and Jacqueline Jackson

Multiple Choice

1. According to the authors, the bikini symbolizes:
    *a. a major public health concern.
    b. the true freedoms of American women.
    c. the cultural repression in the U.S.
    d. sexual freedom for women in the U.S.

Page 213

True/False

2. The authors' main point is that the bikini is as equally repressive as the burka. (False, page 214)

Short Answer/Essay

3. What is the relationship between the burka and the bikini, according to these authors?

Part IV: COMMUNICATION
QUESTIONS ON THE INTRODUCTION TO PART IV

Multiple Choice

1. Difficulty sharing feelings, competitiveness, fear of admitting dependency, and fear of homophobia all contribute to
    a. keeping women from becoming close friends.
    *b. keeping men from becoming close friends.
    c. high rates of alcoholism among men.
    d. Type A behavior.

Page 216

True/False

2. The internet has realized its goal of creating a more level playing field where demographic traits matter less. (False, 216)

Reading 26
FOR THE WHITE PERSON WHO WANTS TO KNOW HOW TO BE MY FRIEND

Pat Parker

Multiple Choice

1. Parker would be put off by a white person who
    a. could stay conscious of Parker's Blackness and her humanness simultaneously.
    *b. would make excuses for Black people who behaved badly.
    c. was relaxed and easy around her.
    d. was aware of Black culture but didn't constantly discuss what she or he knew.

Pages 218

True/False

2. Parker suggests to those who want to be her friend that they allow her to instruct them about Black culture. (False, 218)

Short Answer/Essay

3. Using the model provided by Parker, write an essay or poem addressing the theme of "Advice to a person of a different gender who wants to know how to be my friend."

Reading 27
THE BOY CODE
Everything's Just Fine
William Pollack

Multiple Choice

1. According to Pollack, many boys:
    a. hold the sadness in to the point of suicidal ideas.
    b. hold the sadness in and explode in rage.
    c. act out by taking drugs.
    *d. All of the above.

Page 221

2. According to Pollack, the biggest problem for those who want to help is that:
    *a. we often do not know there is anything wrong.
    b. boys are not good at expressing themselves.
    c. the boys have to reach out first.
    d. boys need professional help.

Page 221

True/False

3. Pollack suggests that ideas about girls and women have changed, while ideas about boys and men have remained constant. (True, page 221)

Short Answer/Essay

4. Why is it so difficult to break through the mask of masculinity?

5. What is the relationship between the mask of masculinity and the boy code?

Reading 28
YOU JUST DON'T UNDERSTAND
Deborah Tannen

Multiple Choice

1. According to Tannen, key issues that contribute to communication differences between women and men are _____ and _____.
    a. size; public status
    b. ethnicity; income
    *c. intimacy; independence
    d. All of the above.

Page 222

2. According to Tannen, frequently when women want _____, men offer _____.
   a. advice; understanding
   b. solutions; parallel situations
   *c. understanding; advice
   d. All of the above.

Page 224

3. According to Tannen, men tend to make decisions without their partners because
   a. they are accustomed to more autonomy.
   b. they feel infantalized to ask their female partners for consultation or permission.
   c. they feel curtailed.
   *d. All of the above.

Pages 222-223

4. According to Tannen, which of the following do women typically NOT want in conversation with intimate others?
   a. Empathy and understanding
   b. Parallel experiences from the other person
   *c. Advice
   d. None of the above.

Pages 224-225

Short Answer/Essay

5. Analyze a relationship you are in according to the issues raised by Tannen. To what extent does that relationship illustrate Tannen's ideas about intimacy, independence, advice, and matching troubles?

6. How does Tannes explain the differences in men and women's needs in conversation?

Reading 29

REAL MEN DON'T CRY ... AND OTHER UNCOOL MYTHS

Phil W. Petrie

Multiple Choice

1. According to Petrie's understanding, men are supposed to possess all the following traits EXCEPT
   *a. powerful emotions.
   b. coolness.
   c. rationality.
   d. objectivity.

Pages 228

True/False

2. Petrie argues, citing various experts, that if true communication is to occur in a couple, both people have to be committed to telling all of their feelings. (False, page 230)

31

3. The fact that staying cool for a Black man is central to a sense of empowerment in a racist social order leads Petrie to conclude that he pursued the correct strategy when he failed to communicate with his wife about their health insurance crisis. (False, page 232)

4. Petrie suggests that Black men can communicate more effectively while still maintaining their "coolness." (False, page 230)

Short Answer/Essay

5. Compare an intimate relationship you are or were part of to the relationship described by Petrie. In what ways does that relationship reflect what Petrie describes?

6. Choose a heterosexual couple you know and discuss how the issues discussed by Petrie affect or do not affect that couple.

7. How does race intersect with gender to affect Petrie's relationship with his wife?

Reading 30
DANNY

Nathan McCall

Multiple Choice

1. Which of the following traits in Danny made it possible for Nate to become friends with Danny?
   a. Danny's willingness to live in a Black neighborhood
   *b. Danny's lack of hesitancy with Nate
   c. Danny's critical analysis of the white establishment
   d. All of the above.

Pages 232-233

2. Which of the following is NOT a reason given by Nate for why he thinks about race all the time?
   a. White women shrinking away from him in elevators
   b. Suspicious white shopkeepers
   *c. The perpetual questions that white people ask him as they try to understand racism
   d. Car door locks clicking as he walks past cars driven by white people

Page 236

True/False

3. After getting to know Danny, McCall is shocked at how little even educated white people know about Black people. (True, page 236)

Short Answer/Essay

4. Consider a friendship you are part of in which you and the other person are different in some important way. Compare and contrast your ways of dealing with differences to those used by Nate and Danny.

5. Based on McCall's description of his friendship with Danny, what are some of the reasons they were able to maintain a friendship across a racial divide?

Reading 31
AMERICAN INDIAN WOMEN
At the Center of Indigenous Resistance in Contemporary North America
M. Annette Jaimes with Theresa Halsey

Multiple Choice

1. A writer quoted by Jaimes and Halsey equates the elimination of American Indians' right to fish with
   a. slavery.
   b. urban poverty.
   c. racism.
   *d. genocide.

Page 239

2. Jaimes and Halsey write primarily about
   *a. the importance of American Indian women in the struggle for American Indian survival.
   b. fishing rights.
   c. armed struggle by American Indian women.
   d. conflict between Hopis and Navajos.

True/False

3. Some American Indian women object to feminism since it serves to impose an agenda that doesn't fit the American Indian struggle. (True, pages 241 and 242-243)

4. Some American Indian women cannot connect to other women of color because they fail to share issues of racial and cultural oppression. (False, page 242)

5. Conflict between American Indian women and white feminists revolves around white feminists' inability to understand the colonization and survival issues facing American Indians. (True, pages 241-242)

6. The authors suggest that native women's alienation from mainstream feminism can prove to be a good thing. (True, page 243)

Short Answer/Essay

7. What is the central issue discussed by Jaimes and Halsey related to American Indians?

8. Under what circumstances do Jaimes and Halsey imagine that white feminists might be able to work with American Indians?

Part V: SEXUALITY

QUESTIONS ON THE INTRODUCTION TO PART V

Multiple Choice

1. One's genetic/biological makeup is the only aspect of sexuality that is
    a. changeable.
    *b. generally immutable.
    c. open to debate in educational reform.
    d. None of the above.

Page 246

2. _____ are considered pathological by the American Psychiatric Association.
    a. Lesbians
    b. Gay men
    *c. Feminine boys
    d. All of the above.

Page 246

3. Some of the reasons why boys who are sexually abused in childhood have a difficult time telling what happened include
    a. fear of being labeled gay if the perpetrator was a man.
    b. the expectation that males are supposed to enjoy sex under any circumstance, if the perpetrator was female.
    c. feeling like a "girl" in the midst of abuse by a man.
    *d. All of the above.

Page 248

4. Research in Latin America has shown that men who have sex with HIV-infected men:
    a. identify as heterosexual.
    b. deny the risks of same-sex unprotected sexual activity.
    c. often transmit AIDS to their female partners.
    *d. All of the above.

Page 249

5. Lesbians and gay men of color or those from small white ethnic communities frequently confront which of the following?
    a. Sexism in their racial/ethnic communities and internalized homophobia in the gay/lesbian community
    *b. Homophobia in their racial/ethnic communities and racism/prejudice in the gay/lesbian community
    c. Internalized racism or prejudice in their racial/ethnic communities and sexism in the gay/lesbian community
    d. All of the above.

Page 249

6. Biological males who appear to be very masculine are always heterosexual. (False, page 246)

7. Psychologist Carla Golden found that some of the college women she interviewed identified as heterosexual but were sexually involved only with women. (True, page 247)

8. Psychologist Carla Golden concluded that the congruence between sexual feelings, behavior, and identity was frequently lacking among the college women she interviewed. (True, page 247)

9. According to Paula Ross, white people can forget about race if they want to. (True, page 249)

Reading 32
HOW MEN HAVE (A) SEX
John Stoltenberg

Multiple Choice

1. Each of the so-called criteria of sexedness is itself a
   *a. continuum.
   b. dichotomized variable.
   c. bipolar distribution.
   d. None of the above.
Page 255

2. Stoltenberg argues that "manhood" is
   a. socially constructed.
   b. a cultural delusion.
   c. a false division unwarranted by human nature.
   *d. All of the above.
Pages 255-256

3. If Stoltenberg had his way, which of the following might become reality?
   a. People could just "have sex" without being concerned about their gender identities, sexual identities, or the sexual characteristics of the person with whom they were having sex.
   b. Women and men would be equal and potentially very similar, apart from bodily differences.
   c. Pornography and other objectification of women would not exist.
   *d. All of the above.

4. Which of the following does Stoltenberg NOT ask of the male college students to whom this essay is addressed?
   a. Choose not to be obsessed with intercourse
   b. Choose not to use drugs or alcohol while having sex
   *c. Choose to be aggressive in sex only if you are pretty sure it is OK with your partner
   d. Choose not to use pornography
Page 261

5. John Stoltenberg, quoting Andrea Dworkin, argues that male and female gender categories are "fictions, caricatures, cultural constructs." (True, page 255)

6. According to Stoltenberg, a fully realized male sexual identity can encompass aspects of female identity. (False, pages 258)

Short Answer/Essay

7. What are Stoltenberg's main points about human sexuality and gender?

8. Stoltenberg argues that maleness is a social construction. What evidence does he use to argue his case? What are the strengths and weaknesses of his argument? To what extent do you agree or disagree with his position?

9. If Stoltenberg had his way, how might the world be different?

10. What advice does Stoltenberg offer college men related to their sexual relationships?

11. What does Stoltenberg mean when he says men use sex to have a sex?

Reading 33
THE MYTH OF THE SEXUAL ATHLETE
Don Sabo

Multiple Choice

1. Sabo's primary focus is
    a. locker-room talk.
   *b. the relationship between sports and sex.
    c. his pain at breaking up with his high school girlfriend.
    d. men's alleged sexual exploits.

Page 263

2. Sabo asserts that to be "manly" in sports, an athlete has to be competitive, successful, dominating, aggressive, stoical, goal-directed, and physically strong. In what situations does he see this definition of masculinity as a problem?
    a. When athletes are injured and cannot maintain this definition of masculinity
    b. When athletes who become fathers have to care for small children
   *c. When athletes apply this definition of masculinity to their relationships with women
    d. All of the above.

Page 264

3. According to Sabo, which of the following is NOT a characteristic of dating as sport?
    a. "Scoring"—having sex without emotional involvement
    b. Sexual relationships are seen as games
    c. Women are seen as opponents to be defeated; man as hunter, woman as prey

*d. The mediating influence of girls in athletics these days

Page 264

4. Sabo argues that the primary cause of the sexual exploitation of women by men is
    *a. patriarchy.
    b. men's resistance to the women's liberation movement.
    c. women's innate inferiority.
    d. All of the above.

Pages 265-266

True/False

5. Sabo argues that in spite of the public stereotype of athletes being virile and sexually potent, many athletes are sexually uptight and fixated on early adolescent sexual antics and exploitation of women. (True, page 263)

6. Sabo argues that there is really no inherent difficulty in men's contradictory needs—on the one hand a need for intimacy from women and on the other their need to act as if they are indifferent to women. (False, page 264)

7. Since young athletes learn about girls primarily from the girls themselves, the information shared among athletes about girls is relatively accurate. (False, page 265)

8. According to Sabo, men seem torn between yearning for excitement and longing for love and intimacy. (True, page 266)

Short Answer/Essay

9. What are the negative links between men's sports and their sexuality, according to Sabo?

10. What changes might Sabo suggest in the structure of sports in order to improve relationships between men and women?

11. Discuss how Sabo interprets sex as a sport. Be sure to address the language he highlights.

Reading 34
USING PORNOGRAPHY

Robert Jensen

Multiple Choice

1. Jensen challenges the notion that
    *a. pornography can only be considered dangerous when social science can prove that it causes harm.
    b. women can enjoy pornography.
    c. men can use pornography and not abuse women.
    d. All of the above.

Page 267

2. In Silbert and Pines's study of 200 street prostitutes, approximately what percentage reported having been raped?
   a. 25%
   b. 50%
   *c. 75%
   d. 97%

Page 270

3. In the study of 900 women by Russell, what percentage of the women reported having been upset because someone tried to get them to do what they had seen in pornographic material?
   *a. 10%
   b. 30%
   c. 50%
   d. 70%

Page 271

4. According to Jensen, men routinely use pornography as an aid in
   a. foreplay.
   *b. masturbation.
   c. rape.
   d. All of the above.

Pages 276-277

True/False

5. Three decades of experimental research on pornography's effects have consistently asserted a link between pornography and violence against women. (False, page 269)

6. Pornography is one part of a sexist system whose messages are reinforced elsewhere. (True, page 269)

7. One use of pornography is to break down the resistance of children to sexual activity with adults. (True, page 274)

8. The accounts of men's use of pornography as reported by Jensen provide proof that pornography causes sexual violence. (False, page 277)

9. Jensen's accounts of men's use of pornography show how pornography is implicated in the abusive behavior of some men. (True, page 277)

10. Jensen's research provides evidence that some pornography consumers have trouble distinguishing between fantasy and reality. (True, page 286)

Reading 35
THE SEX EXPERTS VERSUS ANN LANDERS
Barry A. Bass and Susan R. Walen

Multiple Choice

1. The solution to the dilemma presented by Landers is for men and women to:
    a. tell each other what they want.
    *b. learn their anatomy.
    c. engage in many different forms of "sex."
    d. have more sex.

Page 288

2. According to many sex therapists, "sex" includes:
    a. intercourse.
    b. body awareness.
    c. love and caring.
    *d. all of the above.

Page 288

True/False

3. Sex experts and Ann Landers seem to agree that intercourse is not "where it's at" for most women. (True, page 288)

Short Answer/Essay

4. Why is it important to make distinctions between intercourse and "sex?"

5. Why is it problematic for Landers to make the statement she did regarding women and intercourse?

Reading 36
REPRODUCTIVE RIGHTS
A Disability Issue
Marsha Saxton

Multiple Choice

1. Which of the following does Saxton NOT cover in her article?
    a. Abortion
    b. Adoption
    c. Marriage
    *d. Artificial insemination

2. Saxton argues that:
   *a. people with disabilities should take responsibility for pregnancy and parenthood.
   b. the state should take responsibility for the reproductive choices of people with disabilities.
   c. people with disabilities should adopt children with disabilities rather than have children of their own.
   d. people with disabilities should have a personal care assistant (PCA) to help them raise a child.

Page 292

True/False

3. According to Saxton, in the media there are more disabled characters shown participating in intimate activities. (True, page 290)

4. Saxton argues that children with disabilities (such as retardation) should not be given sexual education. (False, page 291)

5. Saxton does not believe that prenatal screening for severe disabilities should be mandated. (True, page 294)

Short Answer/Essay

6. What are some systemic obstacles people with disabilities face in relation to family life?

7. What is Saxton's argument against prenatal screening?

8. How do stereotypes of people with disabilities contribute to their difficulties?

Reading 37
THE IMPACT OF MULTIPLE MARGINALIZATION
Paula C. Rust

Multiple Choice

1. According to Rust, because homosexuality represents assimilation, it is stigmatized among members of ethnic minority groups in the United States as
   a. a white phenomenon.
   b. a Western behavior.
   c. a white disease.
   *d. All of the above.

Page 296

2. According to Rust, the emphasis on the importance of the family in racial/ethnic communities pressures all individuals to
   a. marry and have children.
   b. resist racial genocide.
   c. pull together to cushion the effects of racism/prejudice.
   *d. All of the above.

Pages 297-298

3. According to Rust, while racism can strengthen commitment to ethnic values and traditions, it can also pressure ethnic minority communities to
   *a. conform to mainstream values.
   b. create new values and traditions.
   c. become politically active in the wider society.
   d. All of the above.

Page 297

4. Monosexism refers to
   a. sticking with one sexual partner for many years.
   *b. always choosing one's sexual partners from the same gender group.
   c. as a bisexual, never being involved with both a man and a woman simultaneously.
   d. All of the above.

Page 298

True/False

5. Ethnic minority bisexuals are under pressure to deny same-sex feelings in order to appear loyal to their ethnic groups. (True, page 296)

6. Since sexual behavior, especially bisexual behavior, is an individual choice and generally private, there is only limited concern that an individual's behavior will reflect badly on one's group. (False, page 297)

7. Ethnic minority bisexuals can always count on the lesbian-gay-bisexual community if they find themselves rejected by their families and ethnic communities. (False, page 298)

8. Ethnic minority bisexuals frequently end up dealing with monosexism in the gay/lesbian community. (True, page 298)

9. Some of Rust's interviewees found that alienation from mainstream culture freed them to understand and/or develop their own identities. (True, page 252)

Short Answer/Essay

10. Discuss some of the obstacles that minority gays, lesbians, and bisexuals face. How are these different from, or similar to, the issues facing white GLBs?

Part VI: FAMILIES

QUESTIONS ON THE INTRODUCTION TO PART VI

Multiple Choice

1. In 1990, approximately what percentage of female college graduates with a child under one year old were in the paid workforce?
   a. 30%
   b. 50%
   *c. 70%
   d. 90%

Page 304

2. In 1992, in approximately what proportion of U.S. families was the husband the sole economic provider for the family?
   *a. 20%
   b. 40%
   c. 60%
   d. 80%

Page 304

3. According to the introduction to this part of the text, one of the most stressful aspects of life for poor families is
   a. finding decent schools for their children.
   b. obtaining affordable health care.
   c. finding a safe place to live.
   *d. the prospect of becoming homeless.

Page 305

4. Approximately what proportion of poor families are headed by white men?
   a. 20%
   *b. 40%
   c. 60%
   d. 80%

Page 305

5. Explicit attention is being paid to _____ these days.
   *a. fathers
   b. poor families
   c. children who come from "broken" homes
   d. working mothers

Page 303

True/False

6. The National Conference of Catholic Bishops has recently urged married couples to move beyond gender stereotypes and develop more equality in marriage, especially when both spouses are employed outside the home. (True, page 303)

7. A major issue for poor families is the constant risk of becoming homeless. (True, page 305)

8. Since poverty is a structural issue that reaches beyond individual families, poverty and homelessness are usually not pathologized. (False, page 305)

9. Sociologists agree that men have begun to share more equally in family life. (False, page 304)

10. A recent careful look at two large surveys of family life suggests that men overreport their participation in housework whereas women do not. (False, page 304)

11. In many states legislation and/or attorneys have arranged for adoptions within same-sex couples. (True, page 305).

Reading 38
THE TRANSFORMATION OF FAMILY LIFE
Lillian B. Rubin

Multiple Choice

1. The major conflict within the couples studied by Rubin was
    a. deciding which in-laws to ask for help with baby-sitting.
    b. figuring which partner would work the night shift.
    *c. negotiating household chores and child care in the home.
    d. All of the above.

2. The Men in Rubin's study cited which of the following as sources of frustration for them?
    a. Not being appreciated for the family work they do
    b. Being victimized outside the home as well as inside
    c. They still feel they must carry the financial burden of the home while their wives do not
    *d. All of the above.
Pages 308-310

3. Researchers cited by Rubin found that in families in which both wife and husband work full-time, women worked about ___ hours a week in household labor while men worked about ___.
    a. 60; 30
    b. 40; 20
    *c. 25; 10
    d. 15; 5
Page 308

4. Among younger couples studied by Rubin,
    *a. more men feel guilty when they don't help with household chores.
    b. household work has become more-or-less equally shared.
    c. children pitch in more with household chores.
    d. men are as likely as women to take charge of arranging child care.
Page 311

5. In Rubin's study, which families appeared the most egalitarian regarding participation in the daily life of the family and involvement with the children?
    *a. African American families

        b.   Asian families
        c.   Latino families
        d.   White families

Page 313

6.   Strategies used by the families studied by Rubin to make ends meet include all of the following
     EXCEPT
        a.   working split shifts.
        b.   leaning on extended family members to provide child care.
     *c.   having the wife stay home to care for the children in order to save day-care costs.
        e.   having husbands pick up overtime work.

7.   Even in families where housework is shared by men, women still:
        a.   are in charge of the emotional life of the family.
        b.   are responsible for the planning of most everything.
        c.   bear the greater burden of chores.
     *d.   All of the above.
        e.   None of the above.

Page 311

True/False

8.   Because of the financial pressure to work more than one job, a substantial minority of men do no
     work at all within the family. (False, page 312)

9.   The fact that some men feel guilty about not helping more in the home leads Rubin to feel hopeful
     about future changes in family roles. (True, page 312)

10. A major challenge for working-class couples is finding time to talk with each other. (True, page
     315)

Short Answer/Essay

11. Name the major struggles faced by the couples studied by Rubin.

12. How have the couples studied by Rubin confronted the challenge of providing adequate childcare
     on a tight budget?

13. Compare and contrast the way the couples studied by Rubin handled household chores and
     childcare to the way your own family of origin handled or handles these tasks.

BLOODMOTHERS, OTHERMOTHERS, AND WOMEN-CENTERED NETWORKS
Patricia Hill Collins

Multiple Choice

1. Collins suggests that cooperative childcare arrangements:
   a. perpetuate stereotypes about Black women as unable to parent.
   *b. serve a critical function in African-American communities.
   c. create divisions among families and fictive kin.
   d. Encourage polygamous relationships.

Page 319

2. What, according to Collins, were factors that have historically contributed to strong African-American communities?
   *a. Slavery, segregation, and racism
   b. Desegregation, drugs, and class-stratified neighborhoods
   c. Slavery, 1980s drug/crime waves, and poverty
   d. Desegregation, racism, and privatization

Pages 320-321

3. Which of the following are at odds with African-American cultural values, according to Collins?
   a. Racism
   *b. Capitalism
   c. Sexism
   d. Divorce

Page 321

True/False

4. Collins argues that men in African-American communities do not participate in childcare activities. (False, page 320)

5. According to Collins, community-based childcare challenges assumptions that children are property. (True, page 322)

Short Answer/Essay

6. Describe community-based childcare in African-American societies. How is it helpful for children, bloodmothers, and the larger community?

7. Consider your own upbringing. Which of the two models that Collins presents most resembles your situation (e.g. traditional, cooperative). Discuss how this method was/was not beneficial no you in light of Collins's discussion.

Reading 40
DILEMMAS OF INVOLVED FATHERHOOD
Kathleen Gerson

Multiple Choice

1. Which of the following is NOT a dilemma faced by the fathers interviewed by Gerson?
   a. Pediatricians who ignore them
   b. Bosses who demand long hours
   *c. Wives who are threatened by the men's involvement with their children and the home
   d. Pressure to earn enough to support the family

2. Men resist full-time child rearing because it
   a. is undervalued.
   b. is isolating.
   c. involves invisible accomplishments.
   *d. All of the above.

Page 325

3. According to Gerson, a widely shared belief that impedes men's ability to function as effective, involved parents is
   *a. skepticism about men's parenting ability.
   b. resistance to allowing daughters to participate equally in activities such as Little League.
   c. children's resistance to being parented by Daddy instead of Mommy.
   d. All of the above.

Page 326

4. According to Gerson, involved fatherhood helps insulate men against
   a. the resentment of wives who want a shared-household arrangement.
   b. divorce.
   c. emotional isolation should a divorce occur.
   *d. All of the above.

Pages 329-330

True/False

5. The forces pulling men into the home are about evenly balanced by those pulling women out of the home. (False, page 326)

6. Fathers who become equal or primary parents tend to be stigmatized. (True, page 326)

7. By focusing on the advantages and discounting the drawbacks of parenting, fathers are able to overcome some of the barriers to equal parenting. (True, page 331)

Short Answer/Essay

8. What are some of the obstacles facing involved fathers?

MAN CHILD
A Black Lesbian Feminist's Response

Audre Lorde

Multiple Choice

1. Lorde discusses some of the challenges of
   a. being a lesbian raising a son.
   b. raising Black children in a racist social order.
   c. the complexity of dealing with male children in women-only events.
   *d. All of the above.

True/False

2. Lorde's son was harassed as much by his peers for being the son of a lesbian as he was for being Black. (False, pages 336, 339)

3. Lorde argues that sons of lesbians face different issues than do other boys. (True pages 334-335)

Short Answer/Essay

4. What are some of the challenges Lorde faced as she raised her son?

Reading 42

I AM A MAN

Raul E. Ybarra

Multiple Choice

1. Which of the following didn't Ybarra do to prove his masculinity?
   a. talk back to his father
   b. stop himself from crying
   *c. hit his girlfriend
   d. try to be like his father

True/False

2. Ybarra's father maintained his control over his family because of his physical size and strength. (False, whole article)

3. Ybarra's mother supported her son standing up to his father. (False, page 343)

Short Answer/Essay

4. Discuss how Ybarra's fear of his father was more than just fear of being abused.

5. How is masculinity tied up with Ybarra's suffering at the hands of his father.

Reading 43
SEXUAL DISSENT AND THE FAMILY
The Sharon Kowalski Case
Nan D. Hunter

Multiple Choice

1. The primary focus of Hunter's essay is
    a. guardianship decisions in court.
    b. legal issues affecting the lives of gay men.
    c. paternity.
    *d. definitions of "family."

Pages 344-345

2. The major issue in the Kowalski-Thompson case was
    *a. the ability of Thompson to maintain contact with Kowalski.
    b. legal challenges for gays and lesbians born with disabilities.
    c. sexual abuse of people with disabilities.
    d. All of the above.

Pages 344-345

3. Hunter argues that in this culture the family represents:
    a. a zone of privacy.
    b. a structure of authority.
    c. a barrier against sexuality unlicensed by the state..
    *d. All of the above.

Page 347

4. According to Hunter, which of the following is likely to be an important legal issue in the next decade?
    a. International adoption by gay and lesbian couples
    *b. Gay and lesbian marriage
    c. Guardianship issues for gays and lesbians
    d. All of the above.

Page 348

True/False

5. Sharon Kowalski and Karen Thompson could not see each other for 3.5 years because Kowalski's father obtained guardianship and prevented Thompson from seeing his daughter. (True, page 345)

6. Parents of lesbians and gays who defend the rights of their children to love whom they want threaten dominant values because they acknowledge that deep family connection can exist even if someone is not heterosexual. (True, page 347)

7. The Supreme Court supported joint custody in the case of a girl born to a married woman whose biological father was not the woman's husband in order to support the child's right to have contact with her biological father. (False, pages 347-348)

Short Answer/Essay

8. Hunter argues that the definition of family is a central issue in U.S. society today. Mention some of the examples she offers to make her case.

9. What are some of the issues raised by the Thompson-Kowalski case?

10. What definition of "family" is implied in Hunter's essay and what do you think of her implied definition?

Reading 44
THE RELATIONSHIP BETWEEN MALE-MALE FRIENDSHIP AND MALE-FEMALE MARRIAGE

Walter L. Williams

Multiple Choice

1. Among North American Indians studied by Williams, men's primary psychological needs were met by
   a. their wives and children.
   b. their wives.
   *c. their same-sex friends from childhood.
   d. third-gender men living as women.

Pages 352-353

2. Williams argues that the idea of homosexuality was essentially not part of the thinking of North American Indians except for
   *a. the role of the berdache.
   b. special same-sex friendships acknowledged by ceremonies.
   c. women who participated in warrior training.
   d. close relationships between old men who had known each other since childhood.

Page 353

3. The structure of marriage in rural areas of Andalusia, Spain, include all of the following EXCEPT
   a. economic arrangements.
   b. food and lodging.
   c. sex.
   *d. meeting the personal intimacy needs of each partner.

Page 354

4. In some rural areas of Andalusia, Spain, according to Williams, men get involved in the rearing of which group of children?
   a. Both girls and boys starting in early childhood
   b. Their sons, starting in early childhood
   c. Both girls and boys starting in adolescence
   *d. Their sons, starting in adolescence

Page 354

5. Williams argues that a major problem in contemporary U.S. marriages is
   *a. the ideal of romantic love.
   b. economic interdependence.
   c. sexual incompatibility.
   d. All of the above.

Pages 355-356

True/False

6. The lack of intimacy and affection between American men illustrates the situation of men's friendships in other parts of the world as well. (False, page 350)

7. There is a vast array of data on men's friendships cross-culturally, if only scholars would pay attention to it. (False, page 350)

8. In some parts of Africa, boys are encouraged to pair up with best friends and participate in friendship commitment ceremonies. (True, page 351)

9. Same-sex friendships among North American Indians studied by Williams were emotionally intense because marriage was not the center of a person's emotional life. (True, page 351)

10. In most human societies, marriage is primarily an economic arrangement. (True, page 352)

11. Though Native American societies did not have taboos against homosexual relationships, they maintained strict gender segregated roles. (True, page 352)

12. A reason given by Williams for lack of family support in contemporary U.S. society is geographical mobility. (True, page 360)

Short Answer/Essay

13. What does Williams recommend related to the structure of marriage in the United States?

14. What is the relationship between American culture's homophobia and failed expectations of marriage?

Part VII: EDUCATION
QUESTIONS ON INTRODUCTION TO PART VII

Multiple Choice

1. "Stereotype vulnerability" as used by Claude Steele can be defined as
   a. the tendency to be vulnerable to public stereotyping in the media.
   *b. the tendency for group members to perform badly when they think their performance is a reflection of their group.
   c. the tendency for white women and people of color to assume that teachers will single them out.
   d. All of the above.

Page 363

2. During the past several decades, the United States has made concerted efforts to bring about
   a. equality.
   *b. equality of educational opportunity.
   c. equality of educational outcomes.
   d. All of the above.

Page 362

3. An effect of eliminating affirmative action in Texas has been
   a. a smaller proportion of students of color in undergraduate school.
   *b. a smaller proportion of students of color in law school.
   c. a lowering of the number of professionals of color entering the work force.
   d. All of the above.

Page 365

4. There are an estimated _____ homeless gay and lesbian youth in New York City.
   a. 2,000
   b. 4,000
   c. 6,000
   *d. 8,000

Page 364

5. According to this introduction, which of the following are expectations in K-12 classrooms?
   a. Being heterosexual
   b. Acting "white"
   c. Acting according to one's gender
   *d. All of the above.

True/False

6. Although most people would like to "help schools teach kids what they really need to learn to succeed," the majority are not willing to work with other racial or ethnic groups in order to make this happen. (False, page 361)

7. Women outnumber men at most colleges, especially higher-status institutions. (False, page 362)

8. The "hidden curriculum" refers to the array of messages that are not part of the course curriculum in schools and colleges, including the differential impact of schooling on different groups. (True, page 363)

Short Answer/Essay

9. What is the difference between equality, equality of educational opportunity, and equality of educational outcomes?

Reading 45

GIRLS AND BOYS TOGETHER . . . BUT MOSTLY APART
Gender Arrangements in Elementary School

Barrie Thorne

Multiple Choice

1. In "Children and Gender: A Construction of Difference" Thorne claims that gender separation among children in schools is:
   a. more severe than what "separate worlds" research has suggested.
   *b. less severe than "separate worlds" research has suggested.
   c. exactly as "separate worlds" research has suggested.
   d. an issue not addressed by "separate worlds" research.

Page 370

2. Barrie Thorne studied
   a. boys and girls in racially mixed middle-class elementary schools.
   b. girls' culture and boys' culture in single-sex elementary schools.
   *c. girls and boys in racially mixed working-class elementary schools.
   d. boys and girls in multiethnic middle schools.

Page 371

3. Which of the following does the "separate worlds" approach to studying gender NOT do?
   a. Emphasize differences between girls and boys
   b. Focus more on boys' groups than on girls' groups
   c. Simplify gender relations among children
   *d. Identify realms in which girls and boys enjoy relaxed interaction

Pages 369-370

4. Which of the following appeared NOT to encourage sex segregation in the schools Thorne observed?
   a. Teachers and aides
   *b. Parents
   c. The students themselves
   d. Administrators

Page 372-373

5. Which of the following is NOT an area of gender overlap described by Thorne?
   a. Rituals of pollution
   b. Chasing

     *c.   Doing homework
     d.   Invasions of gender-specific playground space

Pages 374-378

6. As observed by Thorne, approximately what is the ratio between the amount of space controlled by girls on the playground and that controlled by boys?
     *a.   Girls control about a tenth as much space as boys.
     b.   Girls control about half as much space as boys.
     c.   Boys and girls control about the same amount of space.
     d.   None of the above.

Page 377

7. According to Thorne, adult women who were _____ often speak of adolescence as a particularly difficult time when they were pushed away from participation in _____.
     *a.   tomboys; boys' activities
     b.   sexually active; sports
     c.   sexually abused as children; gender-neutral activities
     d.   None of the above.

Page 383

True/False

8. The tendency among scholars to study boys and girls separately has deepened our subtle understanding of what girls and boys have in common. (False, page 370)

9. The tendency of boys and girls to segregate themselves decreased as the children Thorne studied got older. (False, page 372)

10. A way to put down boys who do not conform to the dominant group is to call them "girls." (True, page 378)

11. Girls are more successful at becoming part of a boys' group than boys are at becoming part of a girls' group. (True, page 380)

12. Boys are more likely to be defined in sexual ways than are girls. (False, pages 378-379)

Short Answer/Essay

13. Compare and/or contrast your own experience on the school playground or cafeteria to that described by Thorne.

14. Consider how Thorne's research findings translate into the adult world. Discuss how you think childhood separation by gender impacts adult life.

Reading 46
DREAMS
Ann Arnett Ferguson

Multiple Choice

1. Being a professional athlete is a viable option for African-American youths because:
    a. it represents the possibility of success.
    b. it makes schooling seem irrelevant.
    c. it allows them to disengage from school's agenda for success.
    *d. All of the above.

Page 387

2. Ferguson gives all of the following as reasons for why there are a majority of African-American youths in jail EXCEPT:
    *a. African-American youths commit more crime.
    b. African-American youths are at a higher risk of being apprehended.
    c. African-American youths are at a higher risk of being charged with more serious crimes.
    d. African-American youths are more likely to be considered dangerous.

Pages 390-391

True/False

3. For African-American youth, sports careers offer successes and affirmation of their identities. (True, page 388)

4. African-American children are much more likely to succeed by trying to obtain high-status occupations through academic channels. (False, page 388)

Short Answer/Essay

5. Discuss some of the links between education and prisons, according to Ferguson.

6. According to Ferguson, what are some reasons why there are more African-American men prison than men of other racial groups?

Reading 47
CONFLICT WITHIN THE IVORY TOWER
Ruth Sidel

Multiple Choice

1. Sidel suggests that _____ is at the root of the conflicts on campus.
    a. ignorance
    b. peer pressure
    *c. entitlement
    d. un-enforced segregation

Page 394

2. According to Sidel, reasons that make racial incidents on campus particularly shocking include
   a. the increasing unacceptability, in the wider society, of overt racism, sexism, anti-Semitism, and homophobia.
   b. the contrast between the expectation of civility in academic settings and the violence of some of the incidents.
   *c. a and b above.
   d. None of the above.
Page 395

3. Some of the issues involved in the definition of date rape include
   a. the use of force or not.
   b. whether a "no" is part of a ritual and doesn't really mean "no."
   c. whether the victim is too drunk or drugged to provide true consent.
   *d. All of the above.
Page 401

True/False

4. According to the Anti-Defamation League, anti-Semitic incidents increased between the late 1980s and early 1990s. (True, page 398)

5. Recently, stranger rape was found to be far more common than acquaintance rape in the United States. (False, page 401)

6. Although date rape and "gang bangs" occur in a wide range of settings, they are most likely to occur at Ivy League schools. (False, page 402)

7. Alcohol and drugs are frequently involved in cases of gang rape. (True, page 402)

8. Sidel argues that more attention has been paid to being politically correct than to hate and violence incidents. (True, page 403)

Short Answer/Essay

9. To your knowledge, has the college you attend experienced any of the kinds of incidents described by Sidel? Describe what has or has not happened.

Reading 48
BLACK AND FEMALE
Reflections on Graduate School

bell hooks

Multiple Choice

1. Which of the following themes does hooks NOT address?
   a. Being a Black woman in predominantly white male graduate programs
   b. Subtle racism within academia
   c. Overt racism in academia
   *d. The intersections of race, gender, and sexual orientation

2. Hooks claims she wrote this essay to:
   a. finally make peace with her experience of graduate school.
   b. avenge the professors that made her experience so difficult.
   *c. provide support for other graduate students in similar situations.
   d. prove that she is an intellectual.

Page 411

True/False

3. According to bell hooks, the presence of increasing numbers of Black professors in predominantly white universities helps to substantially mediate the racism and sexism of the white professors. (False, page 406)

4. Because of the power of racism, black female and black male graduate students tend to have similar experiences in graduate school in English. (False, pages 409-410)

Short Answer/Essay

5. Compare and contrast your own experience as a student with that of hooks, focusing on your relationship with faculty and on how race differences or similarities seem to have affected your experience.

Reading 49

SCHOLARLY STUDIES OF MEN

The New Field Is an Essential Complement to Women's Studies

Harry Brod

Multiple Choice

1. Which of the following is NOT addressed in men's studies, according to Harry Brod?
   a. Critique of traditional scholarship for its androcentric bias
   b. Studying the mutability and diversity of masculinities
   c. Looking at power relations among men
   *d. Focusing only on men

Pages 412-413

2. According to Brod, men's studies is an essential complement to women's studies because
   *a. neither gender can be studied in isolation from the other.
   b. colleges have always taught men's studies.
   c. all feminists agree that this is a good idea.
   d. All of the above.

Page 412

3. According to Brod, the "gender gap" in voting patterns is usually attributed to
   a. changes in men's attitudes.
   *b. changes in women's attitudes.
   c. changes in both women and men.

    d.   changes in the way voting polls are conducted.

Page 412

True/False

4.   Feminists are divided as to the value of men's studies. (True, page 411)

5.   Brod suggests that women-centered perspectives helps asks questions about men. (True, page 414)

Short Answer/Essay

6.   What are the main points in Brod's case in support of men's studies?

Part VIII: PAID WORK AND UNEMPLOYMENT
QUESTIONS ON THE INTRODUCTION TO PART VIII

Multiple Choice

1. At the current rate of progress in closing the income gap between women and men, women will receive equal pay in approximately what year?
   a. 2010
   b. 2025
   c. 2058
   *d. 2083

Page 415

2. Approximately what percentage of U.S. children lives in poverty?
   a. 15%
   *b. 25%
   c. 35%
   d. 45%

Page 415

3. A major cause of diminished income for many people in the United States is
   *a. the shrinking number of high-paid industrial jobs.
   b. a flood of professionals onto the labor market.
   c. high dropout rates from high school.
   d. lack of motivation among the children of middle-class families.

Page 415

4. The percentages of enlisted women and men reporting sexual harassment in the Navy in a recent study are
   a. 12% women, 5% men.
   *b. 44% women, 8% men.
   c. 55% women, 18% men.
   d. 62% women, 20% men.

Page 416

5. According to the introduction, the situation of women workers around the world varies according to:
   *a. the social support offered by governments.
   b. the amount of maternity leave they can have.
   c. their pay.
   d. how industrialized their country is.

Page 417

True/False

6. Although middle-class people have been struggling in the United States, they have essentially been able to maintain the lifestyles to which they were accustomed while growing up. (False, page 416)

58

7. According to Arlie Hochschild, the time bind that many families are in is caused by the corporate culture that pressures people to work long hours. (True, page 417)

8. A person's position in a workplace affects their perception of how fair that workplace is. (True, page 416)

9. The Navy's efforts to establish an equal and fair workplace for all have paid off, as reflected in the equally positive attitudes of various groups within the Navy. (False, page 416)

10. Sociologists Lynn Weber and Elizabeth Higgenbotham found that the majority of white women they studied perceived no race discrimination in their various workplaces, whereas a large majority of Black women did. (True, page 416)

11. The introduction of computers into the workforce has helped women achieve higher status positions. (False, page 416)

Reading 50
IT'S A FAMILY AFFAIR
Women, Poverty, and Welfare
Randy Albelda and Chris Tilly

Multiple Choice

1. AFDC (Aid to Families with Dependent Children) serves about what percentage of the population at any given time?
   *a.   5%
   b.   15%
   c.   25%
   d.   35%
Page 420

2. Approximately how many hours per year do women on welfare spend in the paid labor force? (*Note:* A full-time employee spends about 2,000 hours per year.)
   a.   50 hours
   b.   200 hours
   c.   500 hours
   *d.   1,000 hours
Page 420

3. For many single mothers, AFDC serves the same function as _____ does for higher-paid, full-time workers.
   *a.   unemployment insurance
   b.   medicare
   c.   medicaid
   d.   disability insurance
Page 421

4. Single-mother families are likely to be poor because of

     a.   lack of affordable child care.
     b.   low-paid jobs.
     c.   lack of job flexibility.
   *d.   All of the above.

Pages 421-422

5. Which of the following do Albelda and Tilly NOT recommend to reduce the poverty of women and children?
     a.   Health benefits for low-wage workers
   *b.   A requirement that all women on welfare attend job training or school
     c.   Changes in the tax structure
     d.   Raising the minimum wage

Pages 242-425

6. The U.S. government defines a poverty line as an income below which people are defined as poor. In 1993, approximately what was that income for a family of four?
     a. $7,000
   *b. $12,000
     c. $17,000
     d. $22,000

Page 422

7. The group most likely to be poor in the United States is
     a.   Latino children.
     b.   Black women.
     c.   urban women.
   *d.   Black children.

Page 422

8. One in every _____ children in the U.S. live in poverty.
     a.   20
     b.   2
   *c.   4
     d.   100

Page 425

True/False

9. Most welfare recipients are in and out of the paid work force. (True, page 421)

10. Welfare mothers work significantly fewer hours in the paid work force than do mothers who are not on welfare. (False, page 420)

Short Answer/Essay

11. If you have lived on an income below the poverty line, how does your experience compare to that described by Albelda and Tilly? If you have lived above the poverty line, how might your life change if you or the family that helps to support you were to become poor?

12. What are some suggestions the authors offer as solutions to welfare "reform?"

13. What are some of the assumptions made about AFDC and people on it that hinder its ability to do much good?

Reading 51
SIXTY CENTS TO A MAN'S DOLLAR
Ann Crittenden

Multiple Choice

1. The family wage gap is:
   a. the wage gap that exists for families as they have more children.
   *b. the gap that exists between mothers and non-mothers.
   c. the gap that exists between married couples without children and married couples with children.
   d. None of the above.

Page 428

2. Which of the following is not a strategy used by mothers in the workforce, according to Crittenden?
   a. Starting their own businesses
   b. Choosing more flexible jobs
   c. Doing part-time work
   *d. Opening up day cares

True/False

3. Crittenden suggests parallels between working class mothers and white collar mothers. (True, page 429)

4. Fortunately, many women entrepreneurs are supported by institutional venture capital to get them started. (False, page 430)

5. Crittenden suggests that fathers are given much more flexibility in the workplace. (False, pages 430-431)

6. All 50 states have laws banning employment discrimination against parents, it is just not enforced. (False, page 431)

Short Answer/Essay

7. Consider the dilemmas pointed out by Crittenden that working parents face. Discuss how your own upbringing may have been impacted by parental discrimination. What do you think should be done?

8. What is the family wage gap, and why, according to Crittenden, does it exist?

Reading 52
WHY ARE THERE NO ASIAN ANCHOR*MEN* ON TV?
Ben Fong-Torres

Multiple Choice

1. According to Fong-Torres, factors that appear to contribute to the low number of Asian men in anchor positions include all of the following EXCEPT:
   a. negative stereotypes of Asian men as wimps or gangsters.
   b. acceptable sexualized stereotypes of Asian women.
   c. few role models for Asian men in the TV industry.
   *d. pressure for Asian men to work in radio instead of TV.

True/False

2. According to Fong-Torres, of forty anchor chairs on San Francisco area TV in the late 1980s, only two were Asian men. (False, page 434)

3. One reason why Asian women are more likely to be TV anchors is because they fulfill two equal opportunity slots with one hiring, (True, page 435)

Short Answer/Essay

4. What are some of the explanations offered by Fong-Torres for the low number of Asian anchormen on TV?

5. Name some of the differences between images of Asian men and Asian women that appear to make Asian women more acceptable as TV anchors.

Reading 53
SHARING THE SHOP FLOOR
Stan Gray

Multiple Choice

1. Gray identifies which of the following contradictions in factory culture?
   a. Women's need to work while simultaneously being unprepared and untrainable for the available jobs
   b. The respected role of workers in an economy dependent upon them
   *c. Some men's inability to bond with women workers, even though a united workers' movement would be more powerful
   d. All of the above.

Pages 445-446

2. Gray might best be defined as
   a. an ally in the struggle for women's equality.
   b. a labor organizer committed to both male and female workers' rights.
   c. an educator of men about offensive sexist behavior.

*d.   All of the above.

3. A strategy that Gray found particularly helpful when confronting sexist men was to
    *a.   challenge their manhood.
    b.   reason logically.
    c.   cajole them into agreement.
    d.   threaten firing and transfer.

Page 445

4. Some men resisted the entry of women into the factory because
    a.   they worried about changes in safety conditions.
    *b.   they saw the factory as a sanctum of male culture in which they could be free of responsibilities to women and various forms of social discipline.
    c.   they feared that their wives would not approve.
    d.   they feared a drop in pay.

Page 446

True/False

5. Gray argues that sexist culture undermines working-class solidarity and leaves labor vulnerable to division and exploitation by those more powerful. (True, pages 448-449)

6. Gray argued that many of the women workers had seniority, and this prevailed. (True, page 442)

7. Gray argues that the objectification of women is very different from the objectification of factory workers. (False, page 448)

Short Answer/Essay

8. Name some of the strategies Gray used in order to convince his male coworkers to welcome women workers into the factory.

9. What is the major contradiction addressed by Gray in his essay?

10. Name some aspects of workplace culture that Gray thinks contribute to sexist attitudes.

11. To what does Gray refer when he uses the phrase "playing the foreman at home"?

Reading 54
THE EFFECTS OF AFFIRMATIVE ACTION ON OTHER STAKEHOLDERS

Barbara Reskin

Multiple Choice

1. Reskin offers what kinds of evidence in support of her conclusion that whites' fears of reverse discrimination are exaggerated?
    a.   Employment audit studies of discrimination
    b.   National surveys of incidents of reverse discrimination

c. Analyses of discrimination complaints filed at the EEOC
*d. All of the above.

Pages 453-455

2. Approximately what percentage of whites in national surveys believe that their race has cost them a job or a promotion?
   *a. 9%
   b. 20%
   c. 42%
   d. 66%

Page 454

3. Approximately what percentage of African Americans in national surveys believe that their race has cost them a job or a promotion?
   a. 5%
   b. 18%
   *c. 36%
   d. 57%

Page 454

4. Of approximately _____ reverse discrimination complaints filed with the Equal Employment Opportunity Commission in 1994, _____ were found to be credible.
   a. 1,500; 53
   *b. 7,000; 28
   c. 12,000; 432
   d. 18,000; 1257

Page 454

5. Most whites get their information about affirmative action from
   *a. politicians' and the media's emphasis on quotas.
   b. EEOC workshops in business settings.
   c. orientation to affirmative action provided by affirmative action officers in business.
   d. employee training manuals.

Page 455

6. According to Reskin's review of the literature, what percentage of studies looking at affirmative action and productivity has found a negative effect of the employment of white women and people of color on productivity?
   *a. 0 %
   b. 10%
   c. 20%
   d. 30%

Page 456

7. In policing, the proportions of minority or female officers are _____ to a department's effectiveness.
   a. positively correlated
   b. negatively correlated
   *c. unrelated
   d. None of the above.

8. Which of the following is related to affirmative action in employment?
   a. Favoring under-qualified white women and minorities over qualified white men
   b. Hiring quotas in most workplaces
   *c. Stable or increased productivity
   d. Greatly increased costs related to doing business

Page 456

9. Which of the following is NOT an effect of affirmative action?
   a. Underserved communities receive services, such as when doctors of color practice in communities of color
   b. Some employers voluntarily adopt affirmative action policies
   c. Higher stock prices in firms with effective affirmative action policies
   *d. Decreased productivity in the workforce

Pages 456-458

10. The hiring of a white woman or a member of a minority group over an equally qualified white man is seen as discriminatory by what proportion of the U.S. population?
    a. 5%
    *b. 25%
    c. 45%
    d. 65%

Page 460

11. Most Americans oppose:
    a. affirmative action policies completely.
    b. affirmative action policies for women.
    c. taking race AND gender into account.
    *d. quotas.

Page 460

True/False

12. For many people the most troubling aspect of affirmative action is that it may discriminate against majority-group members. (True, page 453)

13. There is an enormous gulf between whites' perceptions that they are likely to lose jobs or promotions because of affirmative action and the small risk of this happening. (True, page 455)

14. Firms with the best records of hiring and promoting white women and people of color were more financially successful than were those with the worst records. (True, page 457)

15. One way affirmative action plans work is to alter the educational and job requirements for people of color and white women. (False, page 456)

16. The administrative costs of compliance with, and enforcement of, affirmative action are so large as to offset any gains made by more inclusive hiring. (False, page 457)

17. Because of the administrative costs of administering affirmative action, many corporations have refused to comply. (False, pages 457-458)

18. U.S. business leaders have been among those most unwilling to support affirmative action in recent years. (False, pages 457-458)

19. Although most whites oppose hiring quotas, most African Americans approve them. (False, page 459)

20. The kinds of affirmative action practices that most people in the United States support are similar to what most affirmative action employers do. (True, page 460).

Short Answer/Essay

21. Describe how a legal affirmative action program works, according to Reskin.

22. What explains the disjuncture between negative public attitudes toward affirmative action and public attitudes that reflect acceptance of the principles of affirmative action?

23. If you were to try to convince a group of white men that affirmative action is a good thing, how might you structure your argument and what evidence would you use in support of your case? Imagine that many of the white men to whom you are speaking have negative views on affirmative action.

Reading 55
THE GLOBETROTTING SNEAKER

Cynthia Enloe

Multiple Choice

1. Characteristics of countries to which U.S. sneaker manufacturers have preferred to move include those with
   a. suppressed labor organizing.
   b. low wages.
   c. compliant, hard-working women workers.
   *d. All of the above.
Pages 467, 469

2. The actual cost of manufacturing a pair of sneakers that retails for about $70 is approximately _____.
   a. $5
   *b. $15
   c. $25
   d. $35
Page 468

3. According to Enloe, women's labor organizing in Korea accomplished all of the following EXCEPT

66

a. increased wages for women.
b. increased negotiating power.
*c. organizing effectively within male-led unions.
d. consciousness-raising for women's empowerment.

Pages 468-469

4. When sneaker manufacturers moved some factories out of Korea, the newly unemployed women ended up working in which industry?
   a. Auto
   *b. Entertainment (e.g., sex trade)
   c. Garment
   d. All of the above.

Page 470

5. An inherent contradiction in Reebok's decision to place factories in China is Reebok's support for
   *a. workers' rights to organize.
   b. a workplace free of sexual harassment.
   c. affirmative action.
   d. All of the above.

Page 470

6. The workers manufacturing Nike sneakers in Indonesia earn approximately how much per hour?
   *a. 20 cents
   b. $1.00
   c. $2.00
   d. $3.00

Page 467

7. Approximately how many footwear jobs were moved out of the United States in the 1980s?
   a. 20,000
   b. 40,000
   *c. 60,000
   d. 80,000

Page 467

True/False

8. When women demand decent working conditions and a fair wage, they are likely to be threatened with loss of jobs. (True, page 469)

9. Many women factory workers in Korea do not abide by traditional notions of feminine duty and behavior and are organizing resistance strategies. (True, page 468)

Short Answer/Essay

10. What strategies have women workers in Asia used to struggle for higher wages and better working conditions? What kinds of resistance have they faced in the process of fighting for their rights as workers?

Part IX: VIOLENCE

QUESTIONS ON THE INTRODUCTION TO PART IX

Multiple Choice

1. Members of which of the following groups are NOT frequently victims of hate crimes?
   a. Transgendered people
   b. People of color
   *c. White working-class men
   d. Jewish people

Pages 473-474

2. The most serious health risk facing women in the last two decades is:
   a. breast cancer.
   b. heart disease.
   *c. domestic violence.
   d. None of the above.

Page 474

3. Which of the following is NOT typically blamed for violence against women?
   a. The system of gender inequality
   b. Pornography
   c. Men's participation in sports
   *d. The fact that women on average have less education than men

Page 476

4. The growth of law enforcement has affected women of color by:
   a. leading to increased incarceration.
   b. increasing in abuse in prison settings.
   c. denying reproductive autonomy.
   *d. All of the above.

Page 475

True/False

5. African American women were more likely to tell someone of their domestic abuse than white women. (True, page 473)

6. According to Rodríquez, young people join gangs because of the excitement and engagement that accompanies violent activity. (False, page 474)

7. Attention to men and boys as victims of violence has yet to be explored. (False, page 477)

Reading 56
WOMEN, VIOLENCE, AND RESISTANCE
Melanie Kaye/Kantrowitz

Multiple Choice

1. Major reasons why women fail to defend themselves include
   a. the fact that they are frequently dressed in restrictive clothing.
   *b. the beliefs that violence is wrong and violence won't work.
   c. the inability to imagine fighting back.
   d. fear of being more seriously hurt than they might otherwise be.
   Page 482

2. According to Kaye/Kantrowitz, the assumption behind rape is that:
   a. women want to be raped.
   b. men can't help themselves from raping women.
   *c. a man will win in a physical fight.
   d. if a woman fights back the violence escalates.
   Pages 483-484

3. Kaye/Kantrowitz draws parallels between _____ and _____ in their ability/inability to resist violence by others.
   a. welfare mothers; prison inmates
   *b. women; former slaves
   c. female athletes; children
   d. women in the trades; men in female-dominant careers
   Pages 484-485

True/False

4. Rape and sexual violence are relatively low-risk ways of expressing anger in the United States, suggesting profound societal apathy regarding women and children. (True, page 501)

5. Kaye/Kantrowitz argues that men are inherently violent, women inherently nonviolent. (False, pages 486-487)

6. Kaye/Kantrowitz asserts that if women were expected to defend themselves, definitions of male and female would be shaken. (True, page 486)

Short Answer/Essay

7. Summarize Kaye/Kantrowitz's argument in favor of women using guns and other means of self-defense. What do you think of her position?

8. Kaye/Kantrowitz asserts: "Our fear of ourselves then is a fear of ourselves empowered. . . . We are partly afraid we can't be trusted with freedom." Based on evidence that Kaye/Kantrowitz provides, and on evidence from your own experience, what do you think of this assertion?

9. What does Kaye/Kantrowitz predict would happen if women began resisting physical and sexual violence? Do you agree or disagree, and why.

Reading 57
THE KID NO ONE NOTICED
Jonah Blank

Multiple Choice

1. According to psychiatrists, Carneal is:
    a. mentally ill.
    b. mentally retarded.
    *c. ordinary.
    d. suicidal.

Page 494

2. Michael Carneal's reason for the shooting was:
    a. to kill the people who had rejected him.
    b. to avenge being called a "faggot."
    *c. to get people to notice him.
    d. to show his peers that he could not be messed with.

Pages 497

True/False

3. Carneal saw his actions as an adventure. (True, page 496)

4. One of the reasons cited for the shootings was that Carneal's girlfriend had broken things off. (False, page 496)

5. Carneal selected his victims very carefully, striking down those who hurt him most. (False, page 497)

Short Answer/Essay

6. How do expectations about masculinity help explain Carneal's actions?

Reading 58
THE ULTIMATE GROWTH INDUSTRY
Trafficking in Women and Girls
Jan Goodwin

Multiple Choice

1. Among the purposes of United States–based sex tours to the "Third World" listed by Goodwin are
   a. the buying of girls as sexual slaves.
   *b. helping U.S. men find non-feminist brides.
   c. providing a place for soldiers to go while on leave.
   d. All of the above.

Page 500

True/False

2. According to Goodwin, many women from the former Soviet Union have been brought to the United States as sexual slaves. (True, page 498)

3. Within six months of being sold into the sex industry, girls are commonly infected with HIV. (True, page 498)

Short Answer/Essay

4. List some of the ways in which women are exploited in various parts of the world, as described by Jan Goodwin.

5. What values are embedded in the practices of trafficking in women described by Goodwin? Illustrate your answers with examples from Goodwin's essay.

Reading 59
WHERE RACE AND GENDER MEET
Racism, Hate Crimes, and Pornography
Helen Zia

Multiple Choice

1. Zia defines "hate rape" as
   a. the rape of girls of color.
   *b. racially motivated, gender-based crimes against women of color.
   c. rapes that are particularly violent.
   d. All of the above.

Page 503

2. The "Ethnic Sex Challenge" game involved
   a. the rape of a Japanese exchange student.
   b. assault on women of color on ethnic holidays.

*c.   the following of an ethnic checklist by fraternity men in deciding whom to gang rape.
  d.   random selection of a particular ethnic group to target for sexual harassment.

Page 504

True/False

3. Zia recommends that ethnically or racially motivated violent crimes against women be investigated as hate crimes as well as crimes of violence. (True, whole article)

Short Answer/ Essay

4. What does Zia recommend as a legal strategy to deal with violent crimes against women of color?

Reading 60
HOMOPHOBIA IN STRAIGHT MEN
Terry A. Kupers

Multiple Choice

1. Male on male rape is explained as an expression of:
  *a.   dominance.
  b.   homosexual tendencies.
  c.   anger.
  d.   All of the above.

Page 507

True/False

2. The transvestite Kupers found in the prison voluntarily became the "woman" of the prisoners. (True, page 507)

Short Answer/Essay

3. What is the relationship between homophobia and male on male rape in prison?

4. How does Kupers explain bodybuilding in prison?

Reading 61
PHANTOM TOWERS
Feminist Reflections on the Battle Between Global Capitalism and Fundamentalist Terrorism

Rosalind P. Petchesky

Multiple Choice

1. The two main narratives Petchesky addresses in her article as trying to explain 9/11are:
   *a. U.S. cultural imperialism and U.S. democracy and freedom.
    b. U.S. safety and terrorism.
    c. Islamic fundamentalism and Democracy.
    d. global capitalism and war.

Page 509

True/False

2. Petchesky argues that terrorist networks and global capitalism are equivalents. (False, page 509)

3. Petchesky argues that U.S. militarism is about profits and not fighting terrorism. (True, page 512)

4. The U.S. along with Afghanistan are the only two countries that failed to endorse the UN convention on the Elimination of All Forms of Discrimination on Women. (True, page 516)

Short Answer/Essay

5. Discuss Petchesky's suggestions about the symbolism of the phantom twin towers.

6. What are the connections between masculinism and militarism?

7. What are some factors that contribute to the world's ambivalence about U.S. suffering after 9/11?

8. What does Petchesky see as solutions to the dilemma she discusses?

9. This article presents significant insight into the role of the U.S. and imperialism/militarism. How can one negotiate these truths while remaining patriotic?

Reading 62
COMPREHENDING THE AFGHAN QUAGMIRE

Rina Amiri

Multiple Choice

1. In early 1970, women made up _____ of the educational force in Afghanistan.
    a. 10%
    b. 1%
   *c. 60%
    d. 80%

Page 521

2. One of the primary reasons for Afghanistan's situation of perpetual violence and war is:
   a. Islam.
   *b. foreign intervention.
   c. globalization.
   d. oil.

Page 521

True/False

3. According to Amiri, the Taliban promised and delivered law and order to Afghanistan. (True, pages 522-523)

4. None of the suspects in the World Trade Center Attack are Afghans. (True, page 523)

Short Answer/Essay

5. What was the role of the U.S. in the Russian-Afghan conflict?

6. How did fundamentalists from the Muslim world come to power in Afghanistan?

7. What are some of the contradictions in the U.S. war against Afghanistan?

Reading 63
SNEAK ATTACK
The Militarization of U.S. Culture

Cynthia Enloe

Multiple Choice

1. When something becomes militarized:
   a. it appears valueless.
   *b. it appears to rise in value.
   c. it becomes repulsive.
   d. it becomes expensive.

True/False

2. Enloe argues that militarization may prompt some Americans to accept government raids on Social Security to fund the war on terrorism. (True, page525)

Short Answer/Essay

3. How is the U.S. militarizing Afghan women?

4. Why is the American flag a contentious symbol, according to Enloe?

Reading 64
HOW SAFE IS AMERICA?

Desiree Taylor

Multiple Choice

1. According to Taylor, she has never felt safe in the U.S. because:
    a. she lives in a crime ridden area.
    b. she knows how terrorism works.
    *c. she is part of the underclass that is under siege.
    d. she is a woman in a "man's world."

Page 526

True/False

2. Taylor argues that working class people should join with middle class people to be a more unified country. (False, page 528)

Short Answer/Essay

3. How does Taylor connect poverty and the military?

4. Taylor suggests that the appearance of America's bounty is maintained by the exploitation of people right here at home. What does she mean?

PART X: HEALTH AND ILLNESS

QUESTIONS ON THE INTRODUCTION TO PART X

Multiple Choice

1. The fastest-growing group of people with AIDS in the United States is
    *a. heterosexual women.
    b. IV drug users.
    c. gay men.
    d. lesbians.

Page 530

2. Compared to white women, African American women face higher rates of which of the following?
    a. Violence
    b. Childbirth-related illness
    c. Childbirth-related death
    *d. All of the above.

Page 530

3. Approximately how many people are uninsured nationwide?
    a. 10 million
    b. 100 million
    *c. 50 million
    d. 2 million

Page 531

True/False

4. Black and white men die in automobile accidents at similar rates. (True, page 530)

5. Men are more likely than women to commit suicide. (True, page 530)

6. It appears that environmental toxins are linked to male reproductive problems such as testicles that fail to descend. (True, page 529)

7. Whites and Blacks are about equally likely to commit suicide. (False, page 530)

8. White men are twice as likely as Black men to die of prostate cancer. (False, page 530)

9. States that have the strongest restrictions on abortions are more likely to provide resources for children in need. (False, page 531)

Reading 65
MASCULINITIES AND MEN'S HEALTH
Moving toward Post-Superman Era Prevention
Don Sabo

Multiple Choice

1. Female life expectancy is greater than male life expectancy in the United States, Canada, and other postindustrial societies. According to Sabo (citing Waldron), what proportion of this difference can be explained by gender-related behavior?
   a. 25%
   b. 50%
   *c. 75%
   d. 100%

Page 537

2. In a study of adolescents reported by Sabo, traditionally masculine attitudes were associated with all of the following EXCEPT
   a. being suspended from school.
   b. drinking and use of street drugs.
   c. frequency of being picked up by the police.
   *d. lack of condom use.

Pages 538-539

3. Sabo attributes the poorer health of men of color primarily to
   *a. poverty.
   b. racism.
   c. inadequate housing.
   d. All of the above.

Pages 539-540

4. In the 1980s, the number-one killer of Native American men aged 14–44 was
   a. homicide.
   b. AIDS.
   *c. alcohol.
   d. tuberculosis.

Page 540

5. A major health problem in U.S. prisons is
   *a. AIDS.
   b. homicide.
   c. hepatitis.
   d. All of the above.

Pages 541-542

6. Testicular cancer is primarily a disease of
   a. men who are sexually inactive.
   b. hermaphrodites.
   *c. young men.
   d. old men.

Page 543

7. What proportion of male college students report binge drinking?
   a. 10%
   b. 30%
   *c. 50%
   d. 70%

Page 545

8. HIV infection was the _____ cause of death among males aged 25–44 in 1990.
   a. leading
   *b. second leading
   c. third leading
   d. fourth leading

Page 545

9. White males aged 13 and older constituted approximately what percentage of reported AIDS cases in 1993?
   a. 25%
   *b. 50%
   c. 75%
   d. 90%

Page 546

10. Perceptions of people with AIDS are affected by biases against
    a. gay men.
    b. people of color.
    c. poor people.
    *d. All of the above.

Page 546

11. Which group has the highest suicide rate in the United States?
    *a. White men aged 60 and older
    b. Black male adolescents
    c. White women in their fifties
    d. Latina women in early adulthood

Page 547

12. The rate of some level of impotence among men aged 40–70 reported in Massachusetts in the early 1990s was approximately _____.
    a. 10%
    b. 30%
    *c. 50%
    d. 70%

Page 547

13. Which of the following are cited as contributing to patterns of health and illness among men of color?
    a. Economic inequality
    b. Crime
    c. Education
    d. Alcoholism
    *e. All of the above.

Pages 539-540

True/False

14. Sabo argues that aspects of traditional masculinity can be dangerous to men's health. (True, page 535)

15. Male deaths in both the prenatal stage (in utero) and in the first year after birth occur at about the same rates as deaths of females. (False, pages 535-536)

16. Although women live longer, they tend to experience higher rates of illness (morbidity). (True, page 537)

17. Testicular self-examination (TSE) is an effective means of early detection for testicular cancer. (True, page 543)

18. Sabo argues that gay men's commitment to traditional masculinity can put them at risk for illness and death. (True, pages 540-541)

19. The United States has the highest rate of incarceration in the world. (True, page 541)

20. Sabo argues that political and economic changes can enhance men's health. (True, page 548)

Short Answer/Essay

21. What are some of the explanations proposed for the high rate of suicide among men over 60? (Pages 549-547)

22. Sabo argues that men's gender socialization contributes to men's difficulties with health and their shorter life span. Name some of the evidence he cites to argue his case. To what extent do you find his argument convincing?

23. What are the connections between the political, economic and ideological structures of the gender order and men's health?

Reading 66
HEALTH, SOCIAL CLASS AND AFRICAN AMERICAN WOMEN
Evelyn L. Barbee and Marilyn Little

Multiple Choice

1. Which of the following do Barbee and Little NOT name as a health problem affecting African American women at rates disproportionate to their percentage in the U.S. population?
    a. Hypertension
    b. Lupus
    *c. Osteoporosis
    d. Diabetes

Page 553

2. African Americans constitute approximately what percentage of the U.S. population?
    a. 5%
    *b. 12%
    c. 17%
    d. 25%

Page 553

3. Dominant images that Barbee and Little believe interfere with the health and well-being of African American women include all of the following EXCEPT
    a. mammy—faithful, obedient servant.
    b. matriarch—aggressive, strong, independent, unfeminine.
    *c. athlete—strong, resilient, empowered.
    d. welfare mother—unwilling to work.

Pages 555-556

4. The United States and _____ are the only two industrialized countries without a national health insurance plan.
    a. Japan
    b. Italy
    *c. South Africa
    d. England

Page 557

5. In 1988, approximately what percentage of AIDS deaths occurred among African Americans?
    a. 10%
    *b. 25%
    c. 40%
    d. 55%

Page 450

6. Some of the reasons offered to explain the higher mortality rates among African American women with breast cancer include
    a. later diagnosis.
    b. delays in treatment.
    c. less aggressive surgical treatment.

     *d.   All of the above.

Page 559

7.   According to Barbee and Little, lack of full reproductive freedom has resulted in which of the following for African American women?
    *a.   High rates of sterilization
    b.   High rates of adoption of African American children by white families
    c.   Higher rates of cervical cancer
    d.   Higher rates of abortion

Pages 561-562

8.   According to Barbee and Little, hospitals are dangerous places for African-American women because:
    *a.   of a lack of culturally sensitive information.
    b.   most doctors are racist.
    c.   Few doctors are women.
    d.   County hospitals are often in bad neighborhoods.

Page 564

True/False

9.   Barbee argues for a careful examination of the interactive effects of sexism, racism, and classism in the lives of most African American women. (True, page 554)

10.   Images of African American women as sexually promiscuous have contributed to white males' justification of sexual abuse of Black women. (True, page 556)

11.   The lower incidence of breast cancer in African American women can be considered good news in the health of this group. (False, page 559)

12.   In breast cancer treatment, African American women were more likely than Euro-American women to have had surgery. (False, page 559)

13.   Once diagnosed with HIV, African American women are more likely than white women to develop AIDS. (True, pages 559-560)

Short Answer/Essay

14.   Barbee and Little argue that African American women need reproductive freedom. What are some of the elements of the reproductive freedom they propose?

15.   Name some of the violence issues that affect African American women, as reported by Barbee and Little.

Reading 67
REPRODUCTIVE ISSUES ARE ESSENTIAL SURVIVAL ISSUES
FOR THE ASIAN-AMERICAN COMMUNITIES

Connie S. Chan

Multiple Choice

1. Which of the following issues is typically missing on Asian American community agendas?
    a. Child care
    b. Bilingual education
    c. Housing
    *d. Access to reproductive counseling, education, and abortion

Page 569

2. The typical Asian woman for whom Chan interpreted during abortion procedures was
    *a. in her late twenties or early thirties and married with two or more children.
    b. a single college student whose parents did not know that she was having an abortion.
    c. a married woman in midlife who felt she already had enough children.
    d. All of the above.

Page 570

True/False

3. The clinic for which Chan worked provided affordable abortions to its patients in their native languages. (False, page 569)

4. Chan was unaware of the importance of having the choice to receive an abortion until she began working at the clinic. (False, page 570)

Short Answer/Essay

5. What were some of the difficulties faced by Kai Ling, a woman who Chan accompanied to an abortion?

Reading 68

WHY THE PRECAUTIONARY PRINCIPLE?
A Meditation on Polyvinyl Chloride (PVC) and the Breasts of Mothers

Sandra Steingraber

Multiple Choice

1. The byproduct of PVC is:
    *a. dioxin.
    b. oxytocin.
    c. colostrum.
    d. D.D.T.

2. The negative impact of PVC is from:
   a. its direct contact with foods in packaging.
   b. medical products made form PVC.
   *c. its incineration with other trash.
   d. All of the above.

3. Steingraber urges readers to:
   a. consider the benefits of bottle feeding.
   *b. find alternatives to PVC.
   c. not buy food wrapped in plastic.
   d. urge legislators not to incinerate but rather bury garbage.

4. The milk produced in early stages of breastfeeding is:
   a. loaded with antibodies.
   b. contaminated with dioxins.
   c. called colostrum.
   *d. All of the above.

True/False

19. Breast milk is the safest in the first six months of consumption. (False, page 573)

20. The same hormone that controls milk flow in the breast controls orgasm. (True, page 574)

Short Answer/Essay

21. What are the dangers of breastfeeding according to Steingraber?

22. How is it that breast milk can be the most beneficial and the most detrimental to infants?

Reading 69
DOES SILENCIO = MUERTE?
Notes on Translating the AIDS Epidemic

Rafael Campo

Multiple Choice

1. In the U.S., Latino/a account for _____ of the AIDS cases reported to the CDC.
   *a. 1/5
   b. 1/2
   c. 1/8
   d. 1/4

True/False

2. AIDS has been the leading cause of death for Latino men since 1991. (True, page 576)

3. Campo suggests that domestic violence is related to the AIDS epidemic in Latino/a communities. (True, page 578)

4. One of the obstacles towards unifying Latinos to talk openly about AIDS is the very term "Latino." (True, page 580)

5. The image of Latinos as rising stars helps bring attention to the epidemic. (False, page 580)

6. Many Latino men who have sex with men would not consider themselves gay. (True, page 578)

Short Answer/Essay

7. What is the relationship between homophobia and AIDS?

8. How does Latino/a's economic situation contribute to their risk?

Part XI: A WORLD THAT IS TRULY HUMAN

QUESTIONS ON THE INTRODUCTION TO PART XI

Multiple Choice

1. According to Charlotte Bunch, examples of abuse against women that are not typically perpetrated against men and boys include all of the following EXCEPT
   a. abortion of female fetuses.
   b. sex discrimination at work.
   c. lack of control over their own bodies.
   *d. forced labor.

Pages 583-583

2. The "culture of peace" perspective addresses all of the following EXCEPT:
   a. masculine identities.
   b. women's roles.
   c. international war.
   *d. globalization.

Page 583

True/False

3. A current strategy used to address gender injustice is to argue for women's rights as human rights. (True, page 582)

4. People can be politically active and successful without a critical analysis of oppressive aspects of society. (False, page 583-584)

Reading 70

A WORLD WORTH LIVING IN

Roberta Praeger

Multiple Choice

1. Praeger's perspective is influenced primarily by her experiences as
   a. a survivor of maternal abuse.
   b. an incest survivor and college student.
   c. a writer, activist, and businessperson.
   *d. an incest survivor, a single parent on welfare, and an organizer.

2. An effect of single-parenting described by Praeger is
   a. the pressure to organize with other single mothers for cooperative child care.
   *b. isolation.
   c. intense feelings related to childhood abuse.
   d. All of the above.

Page 586

3. Praeger used which of the following strategies to survive depression, suicidality, single-parenting, isolation, and poverty?
   a. Leadership in the incest survivor movement, tenant organizing, therapy
   b. Urban gardening, education, lobbying, organizing
   *c. Organizing work, legislative lobbying, educating others, therapy
   d. Education, group therapy, involvement with a religious institution

Pages 590-591

True/False

4. Praeger found being on welfare to be an empowering experience so she turned to activism. (False, whole article)

5. Turning her anger and guilt about being on welfare inward has helped Praeger survive. (False, page 592)

Short Answer/Essay

6. How does Praeger develop what C. Wright Mills called a sociological imagination—the ability to make sense of one's life in historical and social context?

7. What kinds of empowerment strategies does Praeger find useful in her journey from isolation and depression to community and empowerment?

Reading 71
LA GÜERA
Cherríe Moraga

Multiple Choice

1. What does "la güera" mean in Cherríe Moraga's essay?
   a. The war
   b. The educated one
   *c. The light-skinned one
   d. The Chicana

Page 594

2. As a result of her mother's desire to protect her children from poverty and illiteracy, Moraga became
   a. bilingual and bicultural.
   *b. anglicized.
   c. alienated from her father.
   d. All of the above.

Page 594

3. What is it about Moraga that helped her to understand her mother's oppression and the oppression of other people?
    a. Empathy with her darker-skinned relatives
    b. Her ability to speak English and connect in the Anglo world
    c. Her education
    *d. Her lesbianism
Page 594

4. Moraga argues that what oppressors fear most is
    *a. realizing that they are similar to those they oppress.
    b. united rebellion by those they oppress.
    c. multicultural coalitions in which they will be excluded.
    d. All of the above.
Page 598

True/False

5. A reason why Moraga argues that oppressions cannot be ranked is the reality that lesbians of color belong to two oppressed groups. (True, page 594)

6. Moraga recommends that oppressed people feel their own oppression, keep it conscious, and use that awareness to create alliances with other oppressed people. (True, page 594)

7. According to Moraga, the majority of literature in this country reinforces the myth that what is dark and female is evil. (True, page 597)

8. Moraga argues that women, as victims of sexism, are by definition not oppressors. (False, page 598)

9. A major issue in the women's movement, according to Moraga, is white women's racism. (True, page 598)

10. Moraga admits that she has enjoyed white privilege at the expense of others. (True, page 570)

Reading 72
STOPPING SEXUAL HARASSMENT
A Challenge for Community Education

Robert Allen

Multiple Choice

1. Sexual harassment is
    a. genetically and biologically caused.
    *b. an outgrowth of normal gender socialization.
    c. an occasional and aberrant event—macho behavior gone wild.
    d. rare among professionals.
Page 601

2. When boys and young men resort to _____, they are trying to reduce the girl involved to the level of a dehumanized sexual object with the purpose of keeping her in her place.
    *a. name calling (bitch, dyke, whore, cunt, etc.)
    b. competition
    c. one-upmanship
    d. lying

Pages 602-603

3. Name calling by boys of other boys, using terms like fag, fairy, wimp, sissy, and so on, serves to
    a. push boys to prove they are not what they have been called.
    b. demote unpopular boys to the status of girls or homosexuals.
    c. reinforce the masculine images of what boys expect of each other.
    *d. All of the above.

Page 602

4. According to Allen, a key locus of male power is
    a. men's physical size.
    *b. women's sexual vulnerability.
    c. women's refusal to fight back.
    d. men's hatred of non-masculine men.

Page 604

5. Which of the following does NOT reinforce women's sexual vulnerability to men's power?
    a. Media such as magazines, films, pornography
    *b. Title IX, providing legal support for gender equity in education
    c. Stories of sexual "conquest"
    d. The use of women's bodies in advertising

Page 604

6. The argument that women who postpone complaints of sexual harassment probably enjoy the sexual attention is an example of
    a. sexual stereotyping.
    b. female "gender boxes" as described by Allen.
    *c. blaming the victim.
    d. All of the above.

Page 605

7. Which of the following is NOT an example of how men are hurt by sexism, according to Allen?
    a. Sexism exerts pressure on men to be in control and not express emotion.
    b. Sexism undermines men's intimacy with women and children.
    c. Sexism does not help men's fear of other men.
    *d. Sexism has provoked contemporary rebellion against its repressive aspects.

Page 606

8. Which of the following models of power would Allen like to see supported and developed?
    *a. Power with others to make change
    b. Power over others to make change
    c. Power to assert charismatic leadership that others will want to follow
    d. All of the above.

Page 608

9. By using their experiences as _____, all men have the potential to become allies of women and children.
    a.   victims of violence
    *b.   children
    c.   schoolyard bullies
    d.   parents

Page 608

True/False

10. Although the Hill-Thomas hearings in 1991 drew a lot of attention to sexual harassment at the time, there has been little interest in the issue since then. (False, page 600)

11. In workshops, Allen has found that the tight gender boxes into which his generation was raised are much less applicable to today's youth. (False, page 602)

12. Despite rhetoric of equality, violence is used to keep less powerful groups such as women in their place. (True, page 603)

13. If a woman doesn't protest sexual harassment right away, she probably does not really find it troublesome. (False, page 604)

14. Men have a stake in stopping sexual harassment, abuse, and violence because their female loved ones can be harassed by other men and bring the stress of that experience into men's lives at any time. (True, page 606)

15. Allen argues that African American men, though frequently victimized by white men, still have more in common with men in general than they do with women. (False, page 606)

16. Allen suggests that the "blaming the victim" mentality is restricted to sexual harassment or sexual assault. (False, pages 603-604)

Short Answer/Essay

17. What strategies do Allen and his colleagues use to help young people begin to address gender issues?

18. What evidence and logic does Allen use to attempt to convince men that they should be allies to women and children?

Reading 73
STATEMENT OF PRINCIPLES
The National Organization for Men Against Sexism

Multiple Choice

1. The National Organization for Men Against Sexism wants to challenge
    a. male superiority.
    b. white superiority.
    c. homophobia.
    *d. All of the above.

Pages 610-611

True/False

2. According to NOMAS, traditional masculinity has few redeeming characteristics. (False, page 610)

3. According to NOMAS, the differences between women and men suggest that they should engage in separate struggles for equality, rather than work together. (False, page 610)

Reading 74
DISAPPEARING ACTS
The State and Violence Against Women in the Twentieth Century
Michelle Fine and Lois Weis

Multiple Choice

1. _____ of women killed in the U.S. were killed by a husband or boyfriend.
    a. 20%
    b. 90%
    *c. 60%
    d. 15%

Page 612

2. Over _____ of women entering the New York State prison system have had a history of physical and/or sexual abuse.
    *a. 70%
    b. 90%
    c. 10%
    d. 25%

Page 612

3. According to the authors, _____ and _____ are strategies used by which poor and working class women have been able to interrupt the "cycle of violence."
    a. housing; restraining orders
    *b. welfare; education

     c.   shelters; courts
     d.   police; courts

Page 613

4. Poor and working class individuals are recipients of _____ in the booming economy.
     a.   temporary jobs
  *b.   prisons
     c.   welfare
     d.   factory work

Page 614

5. Poor and working class women are receiving more:
     a.   help from communities.
     b.   flexibility in work arrangements.
  *c.   surveillance.
     d.   food stamps.

Page 615

True/False

6. A woman may be in greater danger once she separates from an abusive man. (True, page 612)

7. Women across racial and ethnic groups are today pursuing formal education to a far lesser extent than are men. (False, page 613)

8. While women constitute only a small fraction of the entire prison population, they are the fastest growing subpopulation. (True, page 614)

9. Since crime and violence are central concerns for poor and working class women, building more prisons is the answer. (False, page 616)

Short Answer/Essay

10. Discuss what the authors mean by "disappearing acts."

11. How do the authors connect cuts to welfare and public higher education to violence in the home?

Reading 75
REPORT FROM JERUSALEM
A Ray of Sunshine within This Long Winter of Violence and Tragedy
Gila Svirsky

Multiple Choice

1. One of the speakers at the rally compared the resistance to Israeli occupation to:
     a.   Nelson Mandela's resistance.
     b.   Chiapas resistance.

c. Martin Luther King Jr.'s resistance.
*d. a and c.
e. All of the above.

Page 619

2. The peace rally included:
a. poetry readings.
b. rock bands.
c. rappers.
e. a torchlight.
*e. All of the above.

Pages 619-620

3. The rally discussed by Svirsky included:
*a. Palestinians and Israelis.
b. only Palestinians.
c. Americans.
d. only Israelis.

Page 620

True/False

4. The coalition of Women for Peace gets very little press in Israel. (True, page 620)

5. Bat Shalom is a women's group. (True, page 621)

Reading 76
ON BEHALF OF THE GLOBAL CAMPAIGN FOR WOMEN'S HUMAN RIGHTS
Charlotte Bunch

Multiple Choice

1. One of the major breakthroughs for the 1993 World Conference on Human Rights was:
a. the consideration of women as part of "human" rights.
*b. recognition of violence against women and girls as a human rights violation.
c. including women in the anti-torture declarations.
d. acknowledgement of women as abusers of human rights too.

Page 622

2. One of the suggestions made several times in this article is for the inclusion of:
a. women as leaders of the UN.
*b. gender sensitivity training.
c. international courts/jails.
d. women included in the concept of "human" rights.

Page 624

True/False

3. One advance made in the international community was a recognition of rape in war as an act of genocide. (True, page 623)

4. While the Vienna Declaration and Programme of Action (VDPA) affirms that the human rights of women and girls are inalienable, extremist interpretations of culture excuse or condone the subordination of women. (True, page 623)

5. Bunch suggests the reallocation of funds from war/defense budgets to feed and house children. (True, page 624)

6. Bunch suggests that it is women's responsibility to end violence against women by speaking out. (False, page 624)

Short Answer/Essay

7. What are some advances in women's human rights that Bunch points out?

8. Bunch highlights six recommendations for action. Choose three and discuss how these could be implemented.

SECTION II
QUESTIONS FOR CLASSROOM DISCUSSIONS, READING JOURNALS, OR TAKE-HOME ESSAY EXAMS

GENERAL INTRODUCTION

1. Define what a sociological imagination is and then use it to answer the following questions about your own life:
   (a) Name a problem you have related to your gender and try to figure out whether it is a personal trouble or a public issue.
   (b) If you had been born thirty years earlier, how might your life have been different?
   (c) What events, trends, movements, and so on, have affected your life? Name at least five. Discuss in detail how at least one of these has affected you personally. Feel free to discuss some of the trends that Disch describes, if they have affected you. Examples: the AIDS epidemic, the women's movement, hate crimes, transgender movement.

2. Have you had the opportunity to study what the author calls dissident voices in high school or college? If so, mention something you learned that has stayed with you and discuss what it was like to learn it.

3. Name some of the ways in which you are privileged and some of the ways in which you are oppressed. How might your life change if you were granted other privileges or faced with other oppressions?

4. In your studies thus far, have you encountered any of the errors in knowledge identified by Elizabeth Minnich? If so, describe. Have you encountered any challenges to these errors? If so, describe.

5. How might you react if friends of yours had a baby and decided to keep the child's sex a secret, choosing, instead, to present the child as a human being?

6. Name a recent experience when you were consciously aware of your gender. What gender rules or values were you aware of in that experience?

7. To what extent are patriarchal systems obvious in your life? That is, which aspects of your life, if any, seem to be controlled by men or male-run institutions?

8. Name a time when you fought back against some form of injustice. How did you come to believe that something was unjust? What did you do in response? Was your resistance to injustice an individual effort or did you work with others? Was gender related in any way to either the injustice you perceived or to your means of resisting it?

PART I: SOCIAL CONTEXTS OF GENDER

1. What is the difference between sex and gender?

2. When various authors say that gender is socially constructed, what do they mean?

3. What kinds of disempowerment have the authors in this section named and what kinds of empowerment strategies do they recommend?

4. Discuss something in one of these readings that moved you, angered you, with which you disagreed, or with which you could identify.

5. Maxine Baca Zinn and Bonnie Thornton Dill suggest a perspective—multiracial feminism—that they believe will help us understand the situation of all men and women. Connect their ideas to two other essays in this part of the text.

6. Identify a place in one or more of the readings where you would like to see more data in order to decide whether or not you would agree with the author's analysis.

7. How might your life be different if you had been born a different sex and of a different race or culture? Use the experience of a couple of this week's authors to guide your exploration.

Reading 1
Manning Marable

8. In what ways is the African American community in crisis, according to Marable? What are some of the causes of this crisis?

9. What kinds of empowerment strategies does Marable suggest in response to the crisis in the African American community?

10. How have race and gender intersected in low-income Black communities to lead to different experiences for women and men, according to Marable?

Reading 2
Helen Zia

11. Do you, or does someone close to you, have similar conflicts with their culture/ethnic heritage and more progressive ideas? How do you (or someone close to you) negotiate those realities?

12. How do you think someone like Zia is able to challenge a traditional upbringing without necessarily alienating family members?

13. Zia talks about "finding her voice" throughout the reading. Discuss the different ways this might have been difficult for her. Also discuss the constant struggle to "keep" her voice in certain situations.

Reading 3

Martín Espada

14. What are some of the stereotyped behaviors that Espada believes he is expected to act out?

15. What does Espada think will be most effective in helping Clemente learn to not live out the stereotypes expected of him?

16. In what ways has Espada "betrayed [his] puppeteers and disappointed the crowd"?

Reading 4

Paula Gunn Allen

17. Why does Allen argue that survival is the central issue confronting American Indian women today?

18. What evidence does Allen offer to support her assertion that the status of American Indian women has declined seriously since their first contact with white people?

19. According to Allen, in what ways have American Indians been pressured to be white?

Reading 5

Ruth Atkin and Adrienne Rich

20. What images, if any, do you hold of what a "Jewish-American Princess" is? How do your images compare or contrast with those presented by Atkin and Rich?

21. To what extent do you find convincing Atkin and Rich's assertion of the connection between anti-Semitism and anti-Asian racism?

22. According to Atkin and Rich, what are some of the issues involved when Jewish women, as members of a historically scapegoated group, are themselves scapegoated?

23. What issues underlie the stereotyping of Jews and other nonmajority groups that appear successful?

Reading 6

Kai Wright

24. How, according to this reading, is life potentially alienating for transgender individuals?

25. Why, in your opinion, is this group of individuals the "one of the most stigmatized populations on the planet"? What does this say about the gender system?

26. How do differences in class impact the experience of being transgender?

27. Do you know anyone who identifies as transgender? What if one of your friends began to openly identify in this way? How would your friendship change, if at all?

Reading 7

Peggy McIntosh

28. Try to add to McIntosh's list of privileges (either white or heterosexual privilege). Was it easy for you to come up with these items, or difficult? Explain why.

29. Do you think that McIntosh's parallel between white privilege and male privilege is fair? Why or why not?

30. Consider the privileges you may have. How can you resist the unearned advantages associated with those privileges? Do you feel that it's necessary to do so in order to create social change?

Reading 8

Maxine Baca Zinn and Bonnie Thornton Dill

31. The word *hegemony* is used several times in the text. What do you think it means?

32. What is your own definition of feminism? How might Zinn and Dill agree or disagree with your definition?

33. How do Zinn and Dill define multiracial feminism and why do they think it's important? What do you think of their argument in support of this perspective?

34. Some people argue that without attention to differences, especially those related to power and inequality, there can be no real understanding and justice among people. Others argue that an overemphasis on differences serves to divide people and make it more difficult to find the common humanity that individuals share. Still others argue for acknowledgment both of differences and of common humanity. Where do you personally stand on this issue and what implications might your position have for the various relationships in your life?

Part II: Gender Socialization

1. Identify a time during the past week when you were particularly aware of your gender. What part do you think socialization played in contributing to your awareness, either on your part or on the part of others involved?

2. Think back to your earliest memory of gender difference. What was going on in that moment? Who was present? What values were attached to what you learned?

Reading 9

Judith Lorber

3. Lorber argues that gender is so ubiquitous that we hardly notice it unless someone does something uncharacteristic of his or her assigned gender. To what extent does this describe or not describe your experience?

4. If there are ways in which you do not conform to gender expectations, name one of them and discuss whether or not your "atypical" gender expression has limited you in any way. Or, imagine doing something uncharacteristic of your gender. How might your friends and family react?

5. Lorber argues that sex is relevant at birth in order to establish a gender category and then doesn't come into play again until puberty (p. 74). What does she mean by this? Can you think of a situation in which sex might be relevant for children between birth and puberty?

6. Following Lorber's suggestion, consider what U.S. society might be like if women were the higher-status gender. What might change? How might your life be different?

7. Imagine waking up tomorrow and finding your sex and gender changed. Imagine going about your day in this new persona. What would be different for you?

8. How do you personally react when you can't tell what gender someone is?

9. Have you ever felt free of feeling gendered? That is, have you ever felt simply human or simply like a person, without awareness of gender? If so, under what circumstances have you felt this way?

10. Lorber argues that gender is socially constructed and that societies socialize women differently in order to keep women subordinate. To what extent do you find Lorber's argument convincing? What else might you want to know before agreeing with her perspective?

Reading 10

Michael S. Kimmel

11. Kimmel argues that men are afraid of the negative judgments of other men. Talk with some men you know and find out whether they think Kimmel's perspective fits their experience. Name the

ethnicity, race, class, and sexual orientation of each man with whom you talk (keep their names confidential).

12. How might you test Kimmel's hypothesis that men are afraid of other men? Discuss briefly how you might design an inclusive study so that men from a wide range of cultural, class, racial, age, and sexual-orientation groups are represented.

13. How might Kimmel's ideas help to explain the experiences of boys as described by Avicolli and Messner?

Reading 11

Michael A. Messner

14. What kind of research method did Messner use and what characterizes this method? What other research methods might be used to study gender among male athletes?

15. To what extent do Messner's findings describe the experiences of men and boys you know?

16. Messner concluded that men's involvement in competitive sports interferes with their ability to be intimate. If you know any athletes, what do you think about his conclusion? How might you gather data that would shed more light on this issue?

17. If Messner is right that for many boys masculinity is developed in the context of sports, how might participation in sports affect the gender development of girls?

Reading 12

Patricia Hill Collins

18. Inventory some of the stereotypes of Black women in various media outlets. How do they conform to or challenge Collins's ideas?

19. How does Collins's reading shed light on the concept of internalized oppression?

20. Discuss the hierarchy that exists between women of color according to the lightness/darkness of their skin.

Reading 13

Judith Ortiz Cofer

21. If you are Puerto Rican or are familiar with Puerto Rican culture, compare Cofer's observations to your own and assess how accurate you find hers to be.

22. Compare the gender norms/rules applied to girls in your own cultural group to those described by Cofer.

23. Have you ever been in a situation in which your behavior was interpreted as a sexual come-on when, in fact, you did not intend to communicate that message? If so, what was that like for you? To what extent might cultural differences explain the miscommunication?

24. Have you ever been treated as a sex object in a way similar to what Cofer describes? If so, what was that like for you and how did you handle the situation?

Reading 14

Tommi Avicolli

25. To what extent is Avicolli's experience similar to the experience of children in schools you attended who didn't conform to gender norms or other norms?

26. Name the various agents of socialization that attempted to make Avicolli conform to gender expectations.

27. What kinds of empowerment strategies did Avicolli use to survive?

Reading 15

Linnea Due

28. What does Due mean by "growing up hidden?"

29. How does Due's story give us insight into gender as socially constructed?

Reading 16

Danny Kaplan

30. Discuss the role of IDF (Israeli Defense Forces) in masculine gender socialization in Israel.

31. Do you feel that the U.S. military has a similar function to the IDF? Why or why not?

32. Discuss the success or failure of IDF as an agent of socialization using Nir's story. (Note: IDF can be successful at some aspects of masculine socialization and not others).

Reading 17
Julie Peteet

33. How are the "rituals of resistance" in the intifada associated with masculinity?

34. Explain the role of violence in the gender socialization of young men in the intifada.

35. Is there anything comparable in U.S. culture, or subcultures, that is similar to Peteet's discussion of the intifada (e.g. gang rituals, fraternity hazings)? Do they have a similar effect? What is the general purpose of these rituals?

Part III: Embodiment

1. To what kinds of physical appearance do you have a positive reaction? To what kinds do you have a negative reaction? Consider faces, hair, muscles, weight, height, presentation of self via clothing or makeup, and so on. How do gender and race or ethnicity affect your judgments? Where did you learn your values related to appearance?

2. In what ways is your own body acceptable to you and in what ways is it disappointing? Where did you learn the values that accompany the judgments you make about your own body?

3. Have you or would you consider plastic surgery to alter your body? If so, under what conditions and for what reasons?

4. How do you relate to the hair on your head and body? How is your approach to your hair related to your gender and your race or ethnicity or culture? Consider not just what you do with the hair on your head but also issues such as shaving, tweezing, and so on.

Reading 18

Elayne A. Saltzberg and Joan C. Chrisler

5. Saltzberg and Chrisler quote Ambrose Bierce at the beginning of their essay: "To men a man is but a mind. Who cares what face he carries or what he wears? But woman's body is the woman." To what extent do you find this to be true in your own circles? How might you study to what extent Bierce's observation holds true?

6. If you are a woman, which, if any, of the attractiveness-enhancing strategies described by Saltzberg and Chrisler do you use and approximately how much time each day do you spend attending to your appearance? If you do not feel comfortable discussing your own behavior, or if you are a man, discuss the appearance-related behavior of someone you know.

7. Saltzberg and Chrisler describe an array of psychological effects of the pursuit of a perfect body among women. How accurate do you think their list is, given the women you know? Do any of the men you know experience similar stress about appearance, body size, and so on?

Reading 19

Becky W. Thompson

8. Thompson argues that eating problems emerge from experiences of oppression such as sexual abuse, racism, and poverty. To what extent does that ring true based on either your own experience or that of someone you know?

9. Thompson challenges the assumption that women develop eating problems because of their obsession with the thinness ideal. What evidence does she use to support her assertion and what do you think of her position?

Reading 20

Brent Staples

10. To what extent does Staples's experience fit the experience of Black men you know? If you cannot answer this question easily, try to interview a Black man and ask him if he has experienced any of what Staples describes.

11. To what extent do you personally tend to stereotype Black men in the ways that Staples describes being stereotyped?

12. How might Kimmel (Reading 13) attempt to make sense of the diverse experiences of Staples and Kriegel?

Reading 21

Leonard Kriegel

13. How has polio affected Kriegel's identity as a man? How might Kimmel explain Kriegel's strategy of coping with polio?

Reading 22

Barbara Macdonald

14. If you are younger than Macdonald, imagine yourself getting old and imagine your body aging in ways similar to those described by Macdonald. How do you think you will feel when that happens? How might your gender affect your reactions to aging? If you already define yourself as old or "older," in what ways have your experiences with an older body been similar to or different from those described by Macdonald?

Reading 23

Christy Haubegger

15. How does your own cultural group deal with round bodies? Is there any support to be other than thin?

Reading 24

Martha Coventry

16. After reading Coventry, what might you advise the parent of an intersex baby to do? What else might you want to know before offering advice?

Joan Jacobs Brumberg and Jacqueline Jackson

17. What is the general statement about the control of (women's) bodies that the authors make here? Do you agree or disagree? Explain your position.

Part IV: Communication

1. Identify a gender-related communication problem you have and talk with some same-sex friends to see whether they share that problem. Report the conversation. To what extent, if any, do others share your problem and to what extent, if any, does your problem seem affected by race, class, culture, or sexual orientation?

2. Identify a race- or culture-related problem in communication that you have had. To what extent does your problem seem related to gender, class, or sexual orientation?

Reading 26

Pat Parker

3. Rewrite Parker's poem and address a hypothetical friend who is a different gender.

4. Rewrite Parker's poem and address a hypothetical friend who is both a different race/culture AND a different gender.

Reading 27

William Pollack

5. Do you have any young boys in your life? Can you see the "mask of masculinity" at work? Does Pollack's writing on this change how you might interact with this (or these) boy (s)? How?

6. How has the "old Boy Code" impacted your life? Can you think of a few examples where this "gender straightjacket" had a negative effect on an experience? Discuss this.

Reading 28

Deborah Tannen

7. Have you ever encountered any of the cross-gender communication difficulties described by Tannen? If so, which ones? If not, how do your communication difficulties or challenges differ from those described by Tannen? How might race, culture, class, or sexual orientation affect your communication difficulties in friendships or with partners?

Reading 29

Phil W. Petrie

8. Have you ever encountered any of the cross-gender communication difficulties described by Petrie? If so, which ones? If not, how do your communication difficulties or challenges differ from those described by Petrie? How might race or culture affect your communication difficulties with partners?

Reading 30

Nathan McCall

9. Describe a friendship or other relationship that you have had with a person whose race is different from your own. To what extent did you directly discuss your racial differences? In what ways was your relationship like or unlike that between Nathan McCall and Danny? If you have never had a friendship with someone of a different race, what do you think has kept you from doing so?

Reading 31

M. Annette Jaimes with Theresa Halsey

10. Name some of the struggles in which American Indian women are engaged, according to Jaimes and Halsey.

11. Name some of the communication problems between American Indian women and white women, as described by Jaimes and Halsey. What would have to happen in order for communication between these two groups to improve?

12. How might the perspective of multiracial feminism help explain the conflict between white women and American Indian women as described by Jaimes and Halsey?

Part V: Sexuality

1. To what extent do your beliefs and values about sexuality emerge from your cultural/racial context?

2. How have HIV and AIDS affected the sexual activity of you and/or your friends?

3. Do you think that Viagra and/or birth control pills and supplies should be paid for by health insurance? Why or why not?

4. In your own life, have you known people whose sexual orientation changed over time? If so, what did the individuals involved seem to be experiencing?

Reading 32

John Stoltenberg

5. How do you react to Stoltenberg's suggestion that humans should just have and enjoy sex without concern about the gender of the people with whom they have it?

6. What do you think of Stoltenberg's advice to college-age men about how to relate sexually with their partners?

7. How do you react to Stoltenberg's assertions about the structure of masculinity? Summarize his position and then share your reactions to it.

Reading 33

Don Sabo

8. If you were raised male, to what extent does Sabo's description of men's sexuality match your own experience? If you were raised female, to what extent does Sabo's description of men's sexuality match your experience with men?

Reading 34

Robert Jensen

9. What is Jensen's justification for approaching the study of pornography as he approaches it? What is your opinion of his approach?

10. What is your opinion of nonviolent pornography? What, if anything, would you like to see done about it?

11. What is your opinion of violent pornography? What, if anything, would you like to see done about it?

Reading 35

Barry A. Bass and Susan R. Walen

12. How do media images of sexual activity and behaviors influence dominant perceptions about what women and men want in sex?

13. Discuss how the focus of the article written by Landers maintains a heterocentric focus on sexuality.

Reading 36

Marsha Saxton

14. Discuss the common assumptions about people with disabilities. Consider gender differences as you do so.

15. Why do you think the social stereotypes of people with disabilities deny them their sexuality? How does this impact their access to reproductive rights?

Reading 37

Paula C. Rust

16. Rust argues that homophobia is likely to be worse in communities of color when those communities are oppressed by the wider white Christian society. Do you find her argument convincing? If so, why? If not, what other kinds of evidence would you want to see before agreeing with her? Do you have any personal experiences or observations that support or contradict her conclusions?

Part VI: Families

1. According to the text, women are working outside the home in larger numbers than ever. Did/do adult women in your family work outside the home and, if so, how does that seem to affect things inside the home? If not, how do you think people in your family would react if women in your family joined the paid work force? What leads you to your conclusion?

2. If you know any families who are poor, what kinds of issues are they facing?

3. Compare or contrast your experiences in your own family with those described by two or three of this week's authors.

Reading 38

Lillian B. Rubin

4. Think about a dual-earner working-class family you know. To what extent do they face (or not face) the kinds of struggles described by Rubin? To what extent do you think the family's race or ethnicity affects how they handle things? Name their race/ethnicity. If you don't know any working-class dual-earner families, compare or contrast your own family to one or more of the families described by Rubin. To what extent do you think your own race or ethnicity affects how your family handles household work and child care?

Reading 39

Patricia Hill Collins

5. Describe the historical roots of African-American community-based childcare.

6. In relation to families in African-American communities, how does the role of Black men differ from that of White men in White communities. How are these roles similar?

7. What are some of the challenges posed to African-American communities that necessitate alternative child rearing?

Reading 40

Kathleen Gerson

8. How involved was your father or father figure(s) in the upbringing of you and/or your siblings? Do any of Gerson's findings ring true in your experience?

Reading 41

Audre Lorde

9. Name some of the wider social realities surrounding Lorde's family that made raising her son a challenge.

Reading 42

Raul E. Ybarra

10. Why do you think Ybarra's father was the way he was? Use your knowledge of gender to explain yourself.

11. The introduction to this section states, "The structures of families reflect gender expectations within particular cultures, and cultures themselves are shaped by surrounding social forces, such as sexism, poverty, and homophobia" (page 303). How does Ybarra's story shed light on this statement?

Reading 43

Nan D. Hunter

12. What do you think of Hunter's conviction that there should be legal protections for gay and lesbian couples?

13. What is your opinion of the Supreme Court decision in *Michael H. v. Gerald D.?* (page 308)

14. If you have gay or lesbian relatives in long-term relationships, to what extent is your relative's partner defined by you (and others) as part of the family?

Reading 44

Walter L. Williams

15. What do you think of Williams's suggestion that men in the United States develop closer friendships with men? Consider in your discussion the fact that his models for male-male friendship emerge primarily from cultures outside the mainstream U.S. culture.

16. Williams argues that it is unrealistic for women and men to get all their emotional needs met in contemporary U.S. marriages. In what ways do you find his argument convincing? To the extent that you do not find it convincing, what kinds of additional data would you like to see?

17. How might Williams's data support the assertions of Kimmel (Reading 13)?

Part VII: Education

1. Compare or contrast your own experiences in K–12 and postsecondary education to those described by some of the writers in this part of the text.

Reading 45

Barrie Thorne

2. If you went to a coeducational elementary or middle school, to what extent do Thorne's observations fit or not fit the school(s) you attended?

3. In what ways did your elementary or middle school teachers teach or reinforce gender differences? In what ways did they encourage your development as a person apart from gender?

4. How might the kinds of schools studied by Thorne affect her findings?

5. What kind of research strategy did Thorne use and what characterizes that strategy? What other research methods might be used in order to learn about gender in schools?

Reading 46

Ann Arnett Ferguson

6. If the educational system is supposed to provide equal opportunity to children, how does Ferguson's argument here contest that?

7. What is the relationship between educational systems and prisons?

8. Did you experience negative labeling in your early school years? How did that impact your experiences?

Reading 47

Ruth Sidel

9. To what extent do the events and experiences reported by Sidel reflect what is happening or what has happened on your own campus?

10. Do you know anyone who has been a victim of acquaintance rape? What were the circumstances surrounding the rape? Who do you think is responsible for what happened?

Reading 48

bell hooks

11. Name some of the ways in which hooks experiences discrimination in graduate school and discuss some of her empowerment strategies. Do you know anyone who has experienced similar kinds of discrimination? If so, describe what happened to the person you know and discuss any empowerment strategies that person used.

Reading 49

Harry Brod

12. How does Brod argue his case for the establishment of men's studies? Do you find his argument convincing? Why or why not? What are some of the potential problems with the establishment of this new field?

Part VIII: Paid Work and Unemployment

1. What kinds of sexual harassment, if any, have you experienced or witnessed in school or in the workplace? If you have not experienced or witnessed any sexual harassment, what might explain that?

Reading 50

Randy Albelda and Chris Tilly

2. Child rearing and housework go unpaid in U.S. society. What would you think of paying people to do this work, or of providing income tax credits or other rewards or incentives to people who perform these tasks?

3. Albelda and Tilly describe an array of recommendations that they think would ease the crisis for poor families and create a more equitable social order. What do you think of their recommendations? Consider each recommendation.

Reading 51

Ann Crittenden

4. What are some of the reasons why working mothers earn less than childless women?

5. How does Critenden's argument support claims made by Collins in her reading about community-based childcare (Part VI)?

Reading 52

Ben Fong-Torres

6. How many Asian men have you seen as anchormen or reporters on TV? What do you think of Fong-Torres's explanation for the absence of Asian anchormen? What additional data might you like to see before accepting or rejecting his explanation?

Reading 53

Stan Gray

7. If you were faced with a situation like Gray encountered in his factory, how might you handle it? Assess the strategies used by Gray and discuss whether or not you would recommend those he tried. If you can think of other ways to approach a similar situation, describe those as well.

8. How might Gray's experience help you handle a situation in which people of color are entering an all-white work setting?

9. Gray describes an all-male environment that is very hostile to women. How do you think this affects the men involved? Are there ways in which this environment might be positive for them? Are there ways in which it might be damaging?

Reading 54

Barbara Reskin

10. Imagine that you meet someone at a party who is convinced that affirmative action has caused a lot of reverse discrimination. Using the data presented by Reskin, describe how you might go about trying to convince the person that she or he is not correct.

11. Where do you personally stand on affirmative action in employment as defined by Reskin?

12. If you were an owner of a corporation, what do you think your position on affirmative action would be likely to be, given the data presented by Reskin?

Reading 55

Cynthia Enloe

13. Try to find out where your sneakers were made and, based on Enloe's data, make a guess as to how much the laborers who made your sneakers were paid.

Part IX: Violence

1. How has violence touched your own life, either directly or because you fear it? How might your life be different without violence or the threat of violence?

2. Name one type of violence and explore what you think causes that kind of violence.

Reading 56

Melanie Kaye/Kantrowitz

5. Kaye/Kantrowitz discusses an array of empowerment strategies—rape crisis centers, hotlines, shelters, and so on—that women have developed in response to male violence against women. Share any experience that you have had with these services or institutions and discuss how effective you think they are.

6. Kaye/Kantrowitz argues that the debate about pornography among feminists sapped energy away from helping stop violence against women. What do you think of her analysis? If you would want more information, what kinds of information would help you decide whether or not her analysis is correct?

7. Kaye/Kantrowitz compares the current subjugation of women in the United States to slavery in the United States. How convincing is her comparison?

8. Summarize Kaye/Kantrowitz's position on women owning and using guns for self-protection. What do you think of the logic and soundness of her argument? Do you agree or disagree with her?

Reading 57

Jonah Blank

9. There have been peer pressure and cliques in schools for decades. Using your knowledge about gender, what about this particular time in history has caused this level of violence from boys?

10. What do you think should be done, if anything, about the alienation of certain students in schools?

Reading 58

Jan Goodwin

11. If you knew anything about trafficking in women before reading Goodwin, what did you know?

12. What do you think should be done, if anything, about the kinds of sexual oppression that Goodwin describes?

Reading 59

Helen Zia

13. Zia argues that some crimes should be prosecuted both as crimes of violence and as hate crimes. What do you think of her position? Do you see any potential risks of doing so?

Reading 60

Terry A. Kupers

14. What is the relationship between masculinity, homophobia, and sexual violence towards men? How does Kuper's discussion help reveal these connections?

Reading 61

Rosalind P. Petchesky

15. Petchesky states, "What we have . . . is an appropriation of religious symbolism and discourse for predominantly political purposes, and to justify permanent war and violence" (511). What does she mean by this? How does she use the metaphor of the twin towers to support this argument?

16. Discuss the connections between the militarism Enloe discusses (Reading 63) and the militarism Petchesky describes. How are they similar/different? How, does this analysis relate to hegemonic masculinity?

17. What is the role of globalization in Petchesky's discussion? How does globalization influence terrorism?

Reading 62

Rina Amiri

18. How much U.S. – Afghanistan history did you know before reading this article? How does this reading help you understand the context in which the attacks of September 11th occurred?

Reading 63

Cynthia Enloe

19. Do you feel that it is necessary to resist militarization? How would one go about doing so?

20. What are your thoughts about the American flag "conundrum?" Do you feel ambivalent about it? Why or why not?

Reading 64

Desiree Taylor

21. What does Taylor mean when she says the U.S. is made up of several countries?

Part X: Health and Illness

1. Compare or contrast the health problems that you or people you know have encountered with those presented by the writers in this part of the text.

2. Identify some of the empowerment strategies—individual or collective—recommended by the writers in this part of the text and discuss how viable you think the strategies are.

Reading 65

Don Sabo

3. Think about the men in your life and compare or contrast their health problems to those presented by Sabo.

4. Sabo argues that the structure of masculinity contributes to men's health problems. What kinds of evidence does he present in arguing his case and to what extent do you find his argument convincing? To the extent that you do not find it convincing, what other data would you need to see in order to be convinced?

Reading 66

Evelyn L. Barbee and Marilyn Little

5. Barbee and Little argue that the position of African American women affects their health in a negative way. What kinds of evidence do they present in support of their position and how convincing do you find their argument? To the extent that you are not convinced, what other data would you need to see in order to be convinced?

6. What do Barbee and Little mean by the differences between reproductive rights and reproductive freedom? Why are these differences important to them?

Reading 67

Connie S. Chan

7. What sorts of social programs or other empowerment strategies might address some of the problems identified by Chan?

Reading 68

Sandra Steingraber

8. As an individual, what do you think you can do to help the situation of PVC and it's toxiv effect on breast milk?

9. According to Steingraber, what is the "Precautionary Principle?" Where else do you think this applies?

Reading 69

Rafael Campo

10. How do ethnicity, class and gender work together to create the silence about AIDS in Latino/a communities?

11. Do you sense that there are similar obstacles to discussing the issue of AIDS in White communities? Explain your thinking.

Part XI: A World That Is Truly Human

1. What do you think of the strategy of arguing for women's rights as human rights as a means to gender justice?

2. Discuss a time when you fought back against injustice of any kind. What kind of strategy did you use? Was it an individual strategy or did you work with others? What kind of success, if any, did your action have?

3. Discuss a time when you fought back against gender injustice. What kind of strategy did you use? Was it an individual strategy or did you work with others? What kind of success, if any, did your action have?

Reading 70

Roberta Praeger

4. Compare or contrast Praeger's experience to that of someone you know who is on welfare.

5. Compare or contrast Praeger's experience organizing for tenants' rights to that of someone you know who has worked for social change.

Reading 71

Cherríe Moraga

6. Moraga names some issues that feminism must address in order to move forward. Name some of them and decide whether or not you think she is correct in her analysis.

Reading 72

Robert L. Allen

7. Allen describes an array of workshops and programs that he and others run through the Oakland Men's Center. How feasible would it be to establish similar programs in an institution near you? Would you like to see that happen? Why or why not?

8. Allen suggests that people need to learn to use "... *power with* others to make change, as opposed to *power over* others to perpetuate domination." (p. 579) Have you ever been part of a process in which you worked with others to bring about change that did not perpetuate domination? If so, describe how that occurred.

Reading 73

The National Organization for Men Against Sexism

9. Share any reactions you have to the NOMAS Statement of Principles.

Reading 74

Micelle Fine and Lois Weis

10. Identify the intersecting oppressions discussed in this article. What is the role of the State in these oppressions?

11. How does the privatization of the economy influence the privatization of the family?

Reading 75

Gila Svirsky

12. Do you identify with the feeling of hope that Svirsky seems to have as a result of this peace rally? Why or why not?

13. Have you been involved in similar activities on your campus or in your community? Discuss these.

Reading 76

Charlotte Bunch

14. How does making women's rights human rights change the concept and enforcement of human rights? Why is it important that these concepts be treated as inseparable?

SECTION III
INTEGRATIVE ESSAY QUESTIONS
BASED UPON READINGS THROUGHOUT THE BOOK

SUGGESTED LENGTH: 6–7 DOUBLE-SPACED PAGES

1. Maxine Baca Zinn and Bonnie Thornton Dill develop a theoretical perspective they call "multiracial feminism." Describe what they mean by this and why they argue for this perspective. Then, discuss at least five other essays in the text and assess whether or not you think the ideas described by Zinn and Dill make sense. Organize your discussion of the other authors around Zinn and Dill's themes, rather than summarizing one essay after another. Consider any of the following essays: Marable, Paula Gunn Allen, Atkin and Rich, Espada, Collins (both articles), Staples, Cofer, Jaimes and Halsey, Lorde, hooks, Sidel, Barbee and Little, Robert Allen, Avery, Zia (both articles), Kaye/Kantrowitz, Goodwin, Taylor and Campo.

2. Michael Kimmel has a lot to say about the relationships of men with each other, focusing on power and powerlessness in men's lives. For example, he redefines homophobia as ". . . fear that other men will unmask us, emasculate us, reveal to us and the world that we do not measure up, that we are not real men" (p. 233). Discuss this and other ideas from Kimmel's essay and, using at least five articles from the text, discuss whether or not you think his ideas make sense. Organize your discussion of the other authors around Kimmel's themes, rather than summarizing one author after another. Include any of these authors: Gerson, Avicolli, Kaplan, Peteet, Pollack, Petrie, Sabo (both articles), Stoltenberg, Ybarra, Gray, Kupers, and Robert Allen.

3. Judith Lorber concludes that " . . . the continuing purpose of gender as a modern institution is to construct women as a group to be the subordinates of men as a group." Using at least five other essays in the text, try to assess her conclusion. What kinds of evidence in the text support her assertion and what kinds seem to contradict it? Finally, what do you think of her conclusion? Be sure to use Lorber's ideas about the social construction of gender as you develop your essay.

4. Many authors in this course refer to the social construction of gender. What do the various authors mean by this and to what extent do you tend to agree or disagree with them? Discuss the following: Lorber, Collins, Williams, Stoltenberg, Kimmel, Messner, Robert Allen, and Thorne.

5. Many authors this semester have challenged the gender system, basing their arguments on various flaws they have experienced or observed in various expressions of gendered behavior in different contexts. Citing evidence from the reading, document some of the ways that the following authors find the gender system unacceptable and name some of the suggestions they make for changing the system. Then, briefly assess these suggestions, based on the authors' arguments and your own experience. Which do you think are viable and which might you personally support? Organize your discussion around themes, rather than summarizing one author after another. Use seven of these authors, plus any others you choose: Robert Allen, Coventry, Williams, Thorne, Kaye/Kantrowitz, Sabo (both essays), Petrie, Gray, Saltzberg and Chrisler, Kriegel, Crittenden, Goodwin, Enloe, Fein and Weis, and Bunch.

6. All-male or mostly male contexts have characteristics that both nurture men and also contribute to men's identities as men. They also have characteristics that have been criticized by many women and men for various reasons. Based on various authors in the text, discuss the pros and cons of these settings from the points of view of the authors. Conclude with your own assessment of various all-male contexts, naming what you personally find positive and/or negative about them.

Use seven of these authors, plus any others you find relevant: Kaplan , Peteet, Gray, Sidel (regarding fraternities), Messner, Sabo (Reading 28), Avicolli, Williams, Thorne, and Pollack. *Note:* Although many of these authors are critical to varying degrees of male socialization in all-male or mostly male contexts, feel free to look for the positive assertions embedded in their essays. For example, although Gray is critical of men's unity against women in his workplace, you might choose to disagree with Gray and read this unity as a positive aspect of male worker solidarity.

7. Pornography and the sexual objectification of women has been addressed by several authors in the course. Discuss various authors' definitions of and views on pornography and sexual objectification of women. Then present any stated or implied recommendations they make regarding it. Finally, discuss your own responses to their suggestions. Are they viable and would you support them? Use evidence from the authors' work as well as your own experience to assess viability. Organize your essay around themes rather than summarizing one author at a time. The authors include Collins, Kaye/Kantrowitz, Stoltenberg, Jensen, Goodwin, Sidel, and Zia.

8. Many authors in the course have addressed the challenge of communicating across gender and other differences. Some have made implicit or explicit recommendations for how to improve communication. Discuss their various recommendations and then discuss your own responses to their suggestions. Are the recommendations viable and do you support them? Use evidence from the authors' work as well as your own experience to assess viability. Organize your essay around themes rather than summarizing one article after another. Choose seven of the following: McIntosh, Jaimes and Halsey, Rubin, Robert Allen, Petrie, Gray, Williams, Espada, Pollack, Moraga, Tannen and Campo.

9. Many authors in the course have addressed empowerment in the face of aspects of the gender system (and other oppressions) that they find dissatisfying. In discussing the empowerment strategies recommended by the following authors, identify what kind of empowerment is recommended and whether it is intended to be practiced at the individual or collective level (see p. 13-14 in the text). Then assess the viability of the strategies based on the authors' evidence and your own experience. Finally, do you support these strategies? Organize your essay around themes rather than summarizing one article after another. Choose seven of the following: Gray, Kaye/Kantrowitz, Robert Allen, Praeger, Zia (both articles), Jaimes and Halsey, Saxton, Ferguson, Svirsky, Enloe and Bunch.

10. Many men in the text are concerned about the ways in which gender socialization has shaped who they have become in ways that they find limiting or frustrating. They either implicitly or explicitly suggest ways to change the gender system in order to give men more options. Using the authors themselves or the men whom they quote or cite, discuss some of these recommendations, assess their viability, and share briefly your own opinion as to which ones you personally would support. Organize your essay around themes rather than summarizing one article after another. Use seven of these authors: Kimmel, Robert Allen, Messner, Sabo, Petrie, Gray, Kriegel, Stoltenberg, Kaplan, Ybarra, Gerson, Rubin, Espada, Williams, Campo, and the National Organization for Men Against Sexism.

11. Imagine that you had been born a different person. Choose a new gender, a new race or culture, and one other change (either a difference of class, sexual orientation or physical ability). Develop a new hypothetical identity based on the readings in the text. Stick to the readings for evidence and avoid any unsupported generalizations about the "new you." In some cases you will have to weave the readings together in a creative way, since not all potential identities are fully addressed. Thus, if you were to imagine yourself as a gay Chicano man, you might say something like: "If I had been born a gay Chicano man, I might have experienced some of the stereotypes described by

Espada," the homophobia described by Avicolli, and the colorism, racism, and homophobia described by Moraga. Use at least six essays in developing your hypothetical identity. Finally, what privileges and liabilities might accompany this new identity, compared to the privileges and liabilities you currently possess?

12. Imagine a world in which the gender system did not exist. Would other oppressions remain the same? How would they be different? Consider the information you have about interlocking oppressions, how would this be different? Use examples provided in various readings to make your point. For example, you might argue that Avicolli's experiences would not have occurred since his suffering was a result of being perceived not masculine enough. You might then argue that homophobia would not persist because masculinity is not a central definer, thereby changing what Messner would have to say about organized sports. Use at least seven readings from this course.

13. This book covers many critical social issues from eating disorders in the U.S. to conflicts in the Middle East. Which do you see as an issue with a practical solution that could be implemented given the resources? How does this issue relate to other ones? How do you think the resolution of this particular issue would impact other situations in need of social change? How would you go about changing it? For example, you might argue that grassroots organizations in Latino/a communities can help educate men and women about safer sex and myths about homosexuality (Campo), and that this, in turn, would potentially shift gender dynamics such that masculinity wouldn't be so intricately tied to homophobia (Messner, Espada) in the culture. You could then go on to discuss other areas, covered in this book, which connect to this aspect of social change (education, violence, work and unemployment). Use at least seven readings from this book.

SECTION IV
INTERNET RESOURCES

Part I: Social Contexts of Gender
Various Fields in Feminism - http://www.cddc.vt.edu/feminism/fields.html

The Men's Bibliography -
http://www.anu.edu.au/~a112465/mensbiblio/mensbibliomenu.html

Part II: Gender Socialization
Gender Public Advocacy Coalition (GPAC) - http://www.gpac.org/

Masculinity and Sports - http://www.aafla.org/9arr/ResearchReports/boystomen.pdf

Part III: Embodiment
Intersex Society of North America - http://isna.org/

Lara Croft and Feminism (on the body) -
http://www.frauenuni.de/students/gendering/lara/home.html

Part IV: Communication
The Communication Initiative - http://www.comminit.com/

National Communication Association: How Americans Communicate -
http://www.natcom.org/research/Poll/how_americans_communicate.htm

Part V: Sexuality
Society for the Scientific Study of Sexuality - http://www.ssc.wisc.edu/ssss/

Queer Resources Directory - http://www.qrd.org/QRD/

Part VI: Families
Kearl's Guide to the Sociology of the Family -
http://www.trinity.edu/~mkearl/family.html

Resources for Family Sociology - http://www.familydiscussions.com/

Part VII: Education
Research on Gender and Education - http://www.aauw.org/2000/research.html

Education and Gender Differences -
http://serendip.brynmawr.edu/sci_edu/education/genderdiff.html

Part VIII: Paid Work and Unemployment
American Public Human Services Association - http://www.aphsa.org/

National Jobs for All Coalition – www.njfac.org/jobnews.html

Welfare Information Network – www.welfareinfo.org

Part IX: Violence
End Violence Against Women Information and Resources -
http://www.endvaw.org/index.htm

National Sexual Violence Resource Center - http://www.nsvrc.org/

Part X: Health and Illness
AIDS Education Global Information System (AEGIS) -
http://www.aegis.com/search/default.asp

Center for Health and Gender Equity (CHANGE) - http://www.genderhealth.org/

Part XI: A World That is Truly Human
National Organization for Men Against Sexism (NOMAS) - http://www.nomas.org/

Feminist Activist Resources on the Net - http://www.igc.apc.org/women/feminist.html

Please also refer to McGraw-Hill's extensive website for further resources on race/class/gender/sexuality: http://www.mhhe.com/raceclassgender